COASTAL NEW ENGLAND SUMMERTIME COOKING

Second Edition

By
Sherri Eldridge

Illustrations by
Robert Groves
Nadine Pranckunas

The gratitude of the author is extended to the Maine Chapter of the American Heart Association for the guidance and information provided. The use of the Association's name to convey the goals of this series of books is also gratefully appreciated. For each book sold the publisher makes a contribution to the American Heart Association to further their life-preserving efforts of research and education.

Coastal New England Summertime Cooking
by Sherri Eldridge
Published by Harvest Hill Press

For additional copies of the cookbooks in this series:

Coastal New England Spring Cooking *Coastal New England Summertime Cooking*
Coastal New England Fall Harvest Cooking *Coastal New England Winterfare & Holiday Cooking*

send $13.95 per book (Maine residents add state sales tax)
plus shipping of $2.00 for the first book and $1.00 for each additional book to publisher:

Harvest Hill Press, P.O. Box 55, Salisbury Cove, Maine 04672
VISA and Master Card are accepted. Credit card orders may call (207) 288-8900.

ISBN: 1-886862-10-9 (Second Edition)   PRINTED IN THE U.S.A.

First Printing: March 1995
Second Printing: June 1995 (Revised)
Third Printing: September 1996
Fourth Printing: September 1997 (Second Edition)
Fifth Printing: May 1998

20% TOTAL RECYCLED FIBER
20% POST-CONSUMER FIBER

PREFACE

The magnificent harvests of summer spark the imagination of everyone, especially those who love to cook, and those who live to eat. This cookbook presents a variety of seasonally fresh recipes, borne of coastal New England vegetables, fruits and gifts from the sea. There are summertime traditions for festive gatherings, and quick and cool preparations suitable for taking to the beach or setting out on a buffet. Whatever your calendar holds, plan on enjoying coastal New England's rich array of tempting recipes.

With the publication of this second edition, a nutritional analysis has been added to help meet your dietary goals. The American Heart Association has developed sound guidelines to assist in the prevention of heart disease, and living a long and healthy life. A pleasurable diet, low in fats and meats, and high in seasonally fresh vegetables, fruits, fishes and grains has also been shown to have numerous other health benefits.

These recipes have been adapted to meet the guidelines of the American Heart Association for healthy adults. Although all recipes are reduced in fat and cholesterol, those such as chocolate desserts should not be eaten every day, but enjoyed once or twice a week. A heart-healthy diet includes diverse and good-tasting dishes that are reasonably low in fat, served in average size proportions, employing common sense meal plans, and regular exercise.

The Hints and References section has specific guidelines for a heart-healthy diet. Also shown is data on the fats and cholesterol found in oils. Although the sodium and sugars in these recipes has been reduced or removed, people on strict diets should adapt recipes to their individual needs.

Please take a few minutes and explore the resources in this book. It has been carefully written to offer you the best of Coastal New England Cooking.

This book is dedicated with love to my mother,

Fran Goldberg,

who for many years did all her cooking while three little girls

(with a total of 30 tasting fingers)

were perched on chairs around her.

The Coastal New England Cookbook Collection follows the American Heart Association Guidelines for Healthy Adults. These wonderful recipes will help make following the American Heart Association guidelines easier and more fun for you by supplying flavorful reduced fat/salt menu ideas using ingredients from your shelves.

...Beth Davis, R.D. M.Ed.

Beth Davis is a Registered Dietician and former member of the American Heart Association's Speaker's Bureau and Heart Health Education of the Young Task Force.

CREDITS:

Cover: "Fruit Market" cotton print, gratefully used as a courtesy of:
Hoffman International Fabrics

Cover: "Spring Garden" floral cotton print, gratefully used as a courtesy of:
South Sea Imports

Cover Designs, Layout and Typesetting: Sherri Eldridge

Front Cover Nautical and Back Cover Watercolors, Chapter Title Page Art:
Robert Groves, Brooksville, Maine

Text Line Sketches: Robert Groves and Nadine Pranckunas

Proofreading: Jerry Goldberg, Marcie Correa, Bill Eldridge and Eleanor Rhinelander

Support, Patience and Recipes: Bill Eldridge, Fran Goldberg, The LeForestiers, Annie Shaw and the Women's Business Development Corporation.

CONTENTS

Breakfast
and
Fresh Fruits

CONTENTS

For other breakfast foods, please refer to the chapters
"Breads and Baked Goods" and "Desserts and Sweets."

Whipped Apricot Creme

4 fresh apricots or peaches
1 cup fresh melon or
     pineapple pieces
1 banana
$1/_2$ cup honey
2 cups non-fat plain yogurt
fresh fruit for garnish

SERVES 4

Poach apricots or peaches for 5 minutes in boiling water. Remove fruit when cool, skin and discard the pits.

Refrigerate poached fruit, melon and banana for 15-20 minutes. Put all ingredients in blender. Process until smooth. Serve in tall glasses with fresh fruit garnish.

Serving: 1/4 Recipe	Calories: 252	Protein: 7 gm
Calories from Fat: 5	Total Fat: 0.5 gm	Dietary Fiber: 2 gm
Saturated Fat: 0 gm	Carbs: 59 gm	Sodium: 90 mg
Component of Fat: 2%	Cholesterol: 2 mg	Calcium: 218 mg

Summer Melon Salad & Lime Sauce

4 cups bite-sized pieces
    cantaloupe, honeydew
    and/or catawba melon
1 cup halved grapes
2 limes
1 teaspoon cornstarch
4 tablespoons sugar
1 tablespoon fresh mint
3 tablespooons chopped
    pecans

Optional:
$^1/_2$ cup fresh chopped figs

SERVES 4

Chill melon, grapes, and chopped figs if desired. Grate 1 tablespoon zest from lime rinds. Squeeze juice of limes into the zest.

In a small saucepan, combine sugar and cornstarch. Slowly whisk in lime juice and zest. Cook over medium-high heat until mixture starts to thicken. Remove from heat. Chop fresh mint into fine pieces and stir into sauce. Cool to room temperature.

Place all fruit in bowl. Pour sauce over fruit and add chopped pecans. Toss lightly. Chill.

Serving: 1/4 Recipe	Calories: 175	Protein: 2 gm
Calories from Fat: 46	Total Fat: 5 gm	Dietary Fiber: 2 gm
Saturated Fat: 0.5 gm	Carbs: 35 gm	Sodium: 16 mg
Component of Fat: 24%	Cholesterol: 0 mg	Calcium: 28 gm

4th of July Wreath: On a straw base, use green florist's wire to wrap bunches of white pearl yarrow, blue cornflowers (bachelor buttons) and red bee balm. Select red-white-and-blue ribbon for bow or loop in spirals around wreath. Small flags, drums and patriotic items can also be stuck into the straw base or glued in place.

COASTAL NEW ENGLAND   SUMMERTIME COOKING

Strawberry-Rhubarb Compote

3 cups strawberries
1¹/₂ cups finely chopped
    rhubarb
³/₄ cup honey or sugar
1 teaspoon vanilla
1 teaspoon lemon juice

SERVES 4

Clean and cut strawberries into quarters. Place chopped rhubard in saucepan with honey or sugar. Cook over medium heat until tender. Add strawberries, cook 7 minutes more.

Remove from heat, stir in vanilla and lemon juice. Serve warm or cold, over waffles, pancakes or with yogurt.

Serving: 1/4 Recipe	Calories: 192	Protein: 1 gm
Calories from Fat: 5	Total Fat: 1 gm	Dietary Fiber: 3 gm
Saturated Fat: 0 gm	Carbs: 48 gm	Sodium: 3 mg
Component of Fat: 2%	Cholesterol: 0 mg	Calcium: 56 mg

Cherry Baked Fruit

$^1/_2$ lb. cherries
1 cup water
1 teaspoon butter
3 tablespoons sugar
1 teaspoon cinnamon
pinch of salt
2 lbs. fresh pears or apples

SERVES 4

Boil cherries in water 30 minutes. Press pulp through large strainer, discard skins and pits. Stir in butter, sugar, cinnamon and salt.

Peel and core pears or apples. Cut vertically, into $^1/_2$-inch thick slices to show shape.

Spray baking pan with non-stick vegetable spray. Place fresh fruit slices on pan and coat with cherry sauce. Set pan on middle rack of oven. Bake at 325° for 25 minutes.

Serving: 1/4 Recipe	Calories: 217	Protein: 1 gm
Calories from Fat: 20	Total Fat: 2 gm	Dietary Fiber: 6 gm
Saturated Fat: 1 gm	Carbs: 53 gm	Sodium: 41 mg
Component of Fat: 8%	Cholesterol: 3 mg	Calcium: 26 mg

Bill's Blueberry Pancakes

In addition to a great pancake recipe,
Billy's Blueberry Pancakes are <u>loaded</u> with blueberries!

SERVES 4

2 cups flour
1 tablespoon baking
    powder
$1/4$ teaspoon salt
2 tablespoons sugar
2 eggs
$1^1/_2$ tablespoons canola oil
2 cups skim milk
$1^1/_2$ cups fresh wild
    blueberries

Sift together dry ingredients. In a separate bowl, beat eggs, then mix in oil and milk. Lightly stir the liquid mixture into the dry.

Reserving juice for Blueberry Maple Syrup, drain canned blueberries, or defrost frozen berries, in sieve. Lightly fold drained blueberries into batter, cook at once.

Serving: 1/4 Recipe	Calories: 405	Protein: 14 gm
Calories from Fat: 76	Total Fat: 8 gm	Dietary Fiber: 3 gm
Saturated Fat: 1 gm	Carbs: 68 gm	Sodium: 1181 mg
Component of Fat: 19%	Cholesterol: 110 mg	Calcium: 374 mg

Blueberry Maple Syrup

MAKES $1^1/_4$ CUPS

1 cup maple syrup
$1/2$ cup juice drained
    or pressed from
    blueberries

Combine maple syrup and blueberry liquid in medium saucepan. Rapidly boil down over medium-high heat for 25 minutes.

Serving: 2 Tablespoons	Calories: 84	Protein: 0 gm
Calories from Fat: 0	Total Fat: 0 gm	Dietary Fiber: 0 gm
Saturated Fat: 0 gm	Carbs: 22 gm	Sodium: 5 mg
Component of Fat: 0%	Cholesterol: 0 mg	Calcium: 33 mg

Whole Grain Hotcakes

1/2 cup sifted all-purpose flour
1/2 teaspoon double-acting
   baking powder
1 cup finely milled whole
   grain flour
2 tablespoons honey
2 cups non-fat plain yogurt
1 1/2 tablespoons canola oil

SERVES 4

Mix flour with other dry ingredients. Combine wet ingredients in a separate bowl. Lightly stir wet mixture into dry mixture. Cook on pre-heated griddle that's been sprayed with oil.

Serving: 1/4 Recipe	Calories: 298	Protein: 12 gm
Calories from Fat: 54	Total Fat: 6 gm	Dietary Fiber: 4 gm
Saturated Fat: 1 gm	Carbs: 51 gm	Sodium: 151 mg
Component of Fat: 17%	Cholesterol: 2 mg	Calcium: 253 mg

Apple-Mint Butter

2 grated apples
2 teaspoons lemon juice
1 cup unsalted whipped
   butter
1/4 cup powdered sugar
1 tablespoon fresh
   chopped mint

MAKES 2 1/2 CUPS

Sprinkle grated apples with lemon juice. Soften whipped butter at room temperature. With a small whisk, blend in sugar, apples and mint.

Serving: 1 Tablespoon	Calories: 39	Protein: 0 gm
Calories from Fat: 34	Total Fat: 4 gm	Dietary Fiber: 0 gm
Saturated Fat: 2 gm	Carbs: 2 gm	Sodium: 1 mg
Component of Fat: 83%	Cholesterol: 10 mg	Calcium: 2 mg

On Hotcakes and Pancakes: Mix the batter just enough to moisten the dry ingredients. Lumps will remain but just ignore them, they'll break up during the cooking process. Test the heat of the pan by dropping a few drops of water on it. The droplets will bounce and sputter if ready for use. If they boil, the pan is too cool. If they vanish, it is too hot.

Vanilla Pecan Waffles

1$^1/_2$ cups non-fat plain
yogurt
$^1/_2$ cup low-fat cottage
cheese
2$^1/_2$ cups white flour
2 cups low-fat buttermilk
4 tablespoons sugar
2 teaspoons vanilla extract
1 tablespoon baking
powder
4 egg whites
3 tablespoons finely
chopped pecans

SERVES 4

Preheat waffle iron sprayed with non-stick vegetable oil.

Process yogurt and cottage cheese in blender until smooth. Add all other ingredients, except egg whites and pecans, blend again. Transfer to mixing bowl. In a separate bowl, beat egg whites into soft peaks, then gently fold into batter.

Ladle batter onto hot waffle iron. Sprinkle chopped pecans over each waffle before closing to cook. Spray waffle iron between waffles to assure a non-stick surface.

Serving: 1/4 Recipe	Calories: 508	Protein: 70 gm
Calories from Fat: 100	Total Fat: 11 gm	Dietary Fiber: 3 gm
Saturated Fat: 6 gm	Carbs: 86 gm	Sodium: 707 mg
Component of Fat: 14%	Cholesterol: 4 mg	Calcium: 457 mg

French Toast

When using real French or Italian bread and soaking overnight in eggs, the crust does not need to be trimmed for French Toast.

12 thick large slices French
   or Italian bread
3 eggs
3 egg whites
1¼ cups skim milk
1 tablespoon vanilla
⅛ teaspoon nutmeg
1 teaspoon sugar
1 tablespoon canola oil

SERVES 6

Place bread slices in deep-dish pan lined with wax paper. Combine remaining ingredients, except oil, and beat. Pour over bread, cover with wax paper, refrigerate overnight.

Preheat frying pan on medium-high heat. Spray with 3 coats of vegetable oil, then lightly brush with canola oil. Fry French Toast on both sides until golden brown.

Serving: 2 Slices	Calories: 224	Protein: 11 gm
Calories from Fat: 55	Total Fat: 6 gm	Dietary Fiber: 1 gm
Saturated Fat: 1 gm	Carbs: 30 gm	Sodium: 390 mg
Component of Fat: 25%	Cholesterol: 108 mg	Calcium: 112 mg

Lemon Honey Syrup

MAKES 1 CUP

1 cup honey
¼ cup water
3 tablespoons lemon juice
1 teaspoon finely grated
   lemon rind

Place honey, water and lemon juice in saucepan over medium-high heat. Cook down for 15 minutes. Stir in grated lemon rind. Serve warm over French toast or waffles.

Serving: 2 Tablespoons	Calories: 65	Protein: 0 gm
Calories from Fat: 0	Total Fat: 0 gm	Dietary Fiber: 0 gm
Saturated Fat: 0 gm	Carbs: 18 gm	Sodium: 1 mg
Component of Fat: 0%	Cholesterol: 0 mg	Calcium: 2 mg

Eggs Benedict Florentine

8 eggs
4 English muffins
1 lb. fresh spinach,
    cooked, chopped and
    well-drained
$^3/_4$ cup water
1 tablespoon cornstarch
2 tablespoons lemon juice
pinch of salt
cayenne (to taste)
1 teaspoon white pepper
2 egg yolks
1 teaspoon unsalted butter

To Serve: Toast English muffins. On each half, place a hot poached egg. Cover with 2 tablespoons hollandaise and spinach.

SERVES 8

Eggs: In a small pot boil 4 inches of slightly salted water. Crack an egg open, swirl water with wooden spoon, and drop egg in center of swirl. Reduce heat, cook 4 minutes. Remove egg, plunge into cold water. Repeat process for other eggs. Just before serving, reheat eggs for 2 minutes in hot (not boiling) water.

Hollandaise Sauce: Boil water in lower pan of double boiler. In the top pan, whisk together $^3/_4$ cup water, cornstarch, lemon juice and spices. Stir constantly and bring to a simmer for 3 minutes. Remove from heat, whisk in 2 egg yolks and butter. Return to heat over boiling water, stir constantly and cook another 3 minutes. Mix in cooked spinach. Keep warm until ready to use.

Serving: 1/8 Recipe	Calories: 177	Protein: 11 gm
Calories from Fat: 162	Total Fat: 7 gm	Dietary Fiber: 2 gm
Saturated Fat: 2 gm	Carbs: 18 gm	Sodium: 278 mg
Component of Fat: 34%	Cholesterol: 270 mg	Calcium: 97 mg

Asparagus & Crab Omelette

1 fresh asparagus stalk,
   cut in $\frac{1}{2}$-inch pieces
1 heaping tablespoon fresh
   crab meat
1 tablespoon white wine
1 large egg
1 egg white
1 teaspoon water
pinch of salt
fresh ground pepper
2 teaspoons grated
   low-fat Swiss cheese

MAKES ONE OMELETTE
Multiply ingredients by number of omelettes.

Lightly steam asparagus and crab in wine. Keep warm over low heat.

Preheat 8-10 inch, non-stick omelette pan over high heat. Whisk egg, white, water, salt and pepper in bowl. Just before pouring eggs into pan, coat thoroughly with non-stick spray oil. Pour eggs into middle of pan ($\frac{1}{2}$ cup at a time if you're whipping up a few omelettes.) Shake and swirl pan to distribute eggs evenly. Set on heat 5 seconds to firm bottom while spreading asparagus, crab and grated cheese over top.

Hold pan by handle and quickly jerk towards you, while tilting far edge over burner. Continue this process and omelette will roll over on itself. When omelette forms at far end, bang on handle near pan to curl edge.

Note: Have spatula handy to assist omelette in its formative stages. An omelette should be cooked in just 30 seconds!

Serving: 1 Omelette
Calories from Fat: 54
Saturated Fat: 2 gm
Component of Fat: 39%

Calories: 142
Total Fat: 6 gm
Carbs: 4 gm
Cholesterol: 230 mg

Protein: 14 gm
Dietary Fiber: 1 gm
Sodium: 422 mg
Calcium: 116 mg

Fresh Cherry Crepes

2 cups all-purpose flour
1½ cups skim milk
1½ cups cold water
4 large eggs
2 tablespoons canola oil
2 cups fresh cherries,
    pitted and quartered
½ cup sugar
2 tablespoons water
2 teaspoons cornstarch
1 teaspoon vanilla extract
½ teaspoon lemon juice

To Serve: Roll each crepe with 2 tablespoons cherry sauce. Dust with powdered sugar or cinnamon.

MAKES EIGHT 8-INCH CREPES

Sift flour before measuring into mixing bowl. Slowly whisk milk and water into flour. Blend until perfectly smooth.   Add eggs and oil. Cover and refrigerate 30-60 minutes.

Simmer cherries and sugar in covered saucepan for 15 minutes. Taste, and add more sugar if needed.   In a small bowl,   blend together cornstarch and water, then mix into cherries. Reduce heat to low, cover, but stir frequently until thickened. Add vanilla and lemon juice. Keep cherries warm while preparing crepes.

Preheat crepe pan on medium-high. Spray with 2 coats of non-stick oil and quickly pour ½ cup batter into middle of pan, tilt to cover. Crepe will be light brown in 30 seconds. Flip, and cook 20 seconds on second side.

Serving: 1 Crepe	Calories: 267	Protein: 8 gm
Calories from Fat: 55	Total Fat: 6 gm	Dietary Fiber: 2 gm
Saturated Fat: 1 gm	Carbs: 45 gm	Sodium: 60 mg
Component of Fat: 21%	Cholesterol: 108 mg	Calcium: 79 mg

Warm Cranberry Pudding

If wheat berries are not available, prepare with freshly made couscous. Start by adding the milk and cinnamon, and continue as shown.

1 cup wheat berries
2 cups washed and
    chopped cranberries
1 cup sugar
1 cup honey
4 cups skim milk
2 teaspoons cinnamon
1 cup chopped dried
    apples
2 teaspoons finely grated
    lemon rind
pinch of salt
1 egg
2 egg whites
1 teaspoon vanilla extract

SERVES 6

Soak wheat berries in water. In a separate bowl, mix cranberries with sugar and honey. Let both bowls sit overnight.

Drain wheat berries, then boil with 4 cups water for 30 minutes, and drain. Add milk and cinnamon. Simmer 35 minutes. Stir in cranberries, apples and grated lemon rind.

Whisk together salt, egg, whites and vanilla. Stir in a small amount of wheat berry mixture. Beat egg mixture into remaining wheat berries. Pour into casserole sprayed with non-stick oil. Bake in 325° oven for 35 minutes.

Serving: 1/6 Recipe	Calories: 430	Protein: 10 gm
Calories from Fat: 15	Total Fat: 2 gm	Dietary Fiber: 2 gm
Saturated Fat: 0 gm	Carbs: 114 gm	Sodium: 148 mg
Component of Fat: 3%	Cholesterol: 39 mg	Calcium: 237 mg

In late summer, look for the bright red cranberries starting to ripen in the fields. Cranberries can easily be added to many baked goods. In addition to their bright color, they add a fresh taste, high fiber and lots of vitamin C. When selecting cranberries, look for plump, firm, rich red fruits, with no signs of leakage or broken skins.

Crispy Breakfast Potatoes

2 egg whites
1 tablespoon chopped
    parsley
pinch of salt
1 teaspoon ground black
    pepper
3 cups finely diced raw
    potatoes
1 tablespoon grated onion

SERVES 4

Mix egg whites and spices in bowl. Add potatoes and onion. Toss to coat well.

Heat frying pan over medium-high heat. Spray thoroughly with 3 coats of non-stick vegetable oil. Pour one-half of the mixture into pan. Using spatula, turn potatoes every few minutes until well browned. Spray pan and repeat frying with remaining potatoes.

Serving: 1/4 Recipe
Calories from Fat: 2
Saturated Fat: 0 gm
Component of Fat: 2%

Calories: 149
Total Fat: 0 gm
Carbs: 32 gm
Cholesterol: 0 mg

Protein: 6 gm
Dietary Fiber: 3 gm
Sodium: 71 mg
Calcium: 39 mg

Southeast Light
on Monhegan Bluffs
Block Island, Rhode Island

No-Oil Granola with Fruit

2 cups quick oats
$^1/_2$ cup wheat germ
$^1/_2$ cup frozen apple juice
   concentrate
1 teaspoon cinnamon
1 tablespoon brown sugar
$^1/_2$ cup golden raisins

SERVES 4

Preheat oven to 300°. Stir together all ingredients except raisins. Spread on cookie sheet. Stirring frequently, toast in oven for about 20 minutes, or until golden brown. Remove from oven and add raisins.

Serving: 3/4 Cup	Calories: 343	Protein: 11 gm
Calories from Fat: 33	Total Fat: 4 gm	Dietary Fiber: 7 gm
Saturated Fat: 0 gm	Carbs: 67 gm	Sodium: 17 mg
Component of Fat: 10%	Cholesterol: 0 mg	Calcium: 48 mg

Breads
and
Baked Goods

CONTENTS

Sweet baked goods are also in the chapter "Desserts and Sweets."
Spreads for bread are located in "Appetizers and Finger Food."

Note: The nutritional analysis for breads is based on 12 slices per bread loaf.

Raisin Bran Muffins

3 cups shredded bran
   breakfast cereal
$^1/_4$ cup canola oil
1 cup raisins
1 cup boiling water
2 eggs
$2^1/_2$ cups low-fat
   buttermilk
$^1/_4$ cup honey
$2^1/_4$ cups all-purpose flour
1 tablespoon sugar
$^1/_2$ teaspoon baking soda
1 tablespoon baking
   powder

MAKES 24 MUFFINS

Preheat oven to 375°. Spray 24 muffin tin cups with non-stick oil.

Combine cereal, oil and raisins in mixing bowl. Add boiling water and stir. In a separate bowl, beat eggs, buttermilk and honey. Add liquid to cereal mixture.

In a small bowl, mix together flour, sugar, baking soda and baking powder. Stir into the batter mixture. Cover and rest 25 minutes. Fill tins three-quarters full, bake 25 minutes.

Serving: 1 Muffin
Calories from Fat: 29
Saturated Fat: 0 gm
Component of Fat: 20%

Calories: 130
Total Fat: 3 gm
Carbs: 24 gm
Cholesterol: 19 mg

Protein: 4 gm
Dietary Fiber: 3 gm
Sodium: 189 mg
Calcium: 83 mg

Blueberry Muffins

$\frac{1}{2}$ cup non-fat plain
yogurt

$\frac{1}{2}$ cup non-fat cottage
cheese

3 eggs

2 cups sugar

2 tablespoons canola oil

1 tablespoon lemon juice

2 teaspoons vanilla
extract

3 cups all-purpose flour

1 tablespoon baking
powder

1 pint fresh wild
blueberries, dusted
in 1 tablespoon flour

MAKES 18 MUFFINS

Preheat oven to 350°. In large mixing bowl blend yogurt and cottage cheese with electric beater for 3 minutes. Add eggs, sugar, oil, lemon juice and vanilla. Beat well. Slowly add flour and baking powder, beat 3 minutes. By hand, gently fold in dusted blueberries.

Lightly spray muffin tins with non-stick oil. Fill tins three-quarters full. Bake 25 minutes, or until a toothpick inserted in center of muffins comes out clean.

Serving: 1 Muffin	Calories: 208	Protein: 5 gm
Calories from Fat: 23	Total Fat: 3 gm	Dietary Fiber: 1 gm
Saturated Fat: 0.5 gm	Carbs: 42 gm	Sodium: 96 mg
Component of Fat: 11%	Cholesterol: 37 mg	Calcium: 48 mg

In Fisher's Island Sound, off Stonington, Connecticut, is an island named Rhodes Folly. After the revolution the state lines of New York, Connecticut and Rhode Island intersected on the island. In 1785, a time of prohibition, James Rhode bought the island and in the spot where the state lines intersected, built a very large saloon. (cont.)

Zucchini & Everything Nice Muffins
These moist muffins have less than 2 grams of fat each!

1 cup sugar
1 cup shredded zucchini
³/₄ cup unsweetened
     applesauce
¹/₂ cup raisins
2 eggs
2 teaspoons canola oil
2 cups all-purpose flour
1 teaspoon baking powder
1 teaspoon baking soda
pinch of salt
1 teaspoon allspice
1 tablespoon cinnamon

MAKES 12 MUFFINS

Preheat oven to 350°. Spray muffins tins with non-stick oil.

In a large bowl, mix sugar, shredded zucchini, applesauce, raisins, eggs and oil. In a separate bowl, combine remaining ingredients. Briefly stir flour mixture into wet ingredients, just until moistened.

Divide batter among muffin cups. Bake for 20-25 minutes or until toothpick inserted in muffins comes out clean. Immediately remove from tins and cool on wire rack.

Serving: 1 Muffin	Calories: 188	Protein: 4 gm
Calories from Fat: 16	Total Fat: 2 gm	Dietary Fiber: 2 gm
Saturated Fat: 0.5 gm	Carbs: 40 gm	Sodium: 161 mg
Component of Fat: 8%	Cholesterol: 36 mg	Calcium: 34 mg

(cont.) The island saloon serviced sailors heading to "dry" land. When liquor officers of a particular state entered the saloon, Rhode moved the liquor into another part of the building, and actually into another state. The authorities of the three states finally got together and came through all the doors at once - hence the island's name,   "Rhodes Folly."

New London Ship's Biscuits

2 cups all-purpose flour
$^1/_2$ teaspoon salt
2 tablespoons canola oil
$^1/_2$ cup water

MAKES EIGHTEEN 2-INCH BISCUITS

Preheat oven to 325°. Spray cookie sheet with non-stick oil.

Mix flour and salt. Use fingertips to work oil into flour. Stir in water to make a stiff dough.

With a rolling pin, pound dough to $^1/_2$-inch thickness. Fold and pound thin again. Repeat 6-8 times, until dough is elastic.

Roll dough to $^1/_2$-inch thicknes, cut into 2-inch rounds with biscuit cutter.   Bake about 20 minutes. Store in tight container.

Serving: 1 Biscuit	Calories: 64	Protein: 1 gm
Calories from Fat: 15	Total Fat: 2 gm	Dietary Fiber: 0 gm
Saturated Fat: 0 gm	Carbs: 11 gm	Sodium: 65 mg
Component of Fat: 24%	Cholesterol: 0 mg	Calcium: 2 mg

New London Harbor Light, Connecticut

Buttermilk Fan-Tans

2 cups low-fat buttermilk
1 package dry yeast
$1/4$ teaspoon baking soda
$1/2$ teaspoon salt
$1/4$ cup sugar
2 tablespoons canola oil
4 cups sifted all-purpose
   flour
1 tablespoon canola oil
   for coating bowl

MAKES 24 ROLLS

Heat buttermilk to 110°, then sprinkle yeast over top. Let rest 5 minutes, then stir to dissolve yeast. Mix in baking soda, salt and sugar. Beat well, then add oil and 2 cups of flour. Stir, and knead in remaining flour. Place dough in bowl that's been sprayed with oil and turn to coat all sides. Cover, put in warm place, and let rise until doubled in bulk. Punch down, and knead 1 minute.

Preheat oven to 350°. Spray muffin tins with non-stick oil. Roll dough into a square, one-eighth inch thick, and brush with oil. Cut dough into $1^1/_2$-inch wide strips and stack strips seven layers high. Using a string to make a sawing motion, cut stacks into $1^1/_2$-inch wide sections. Put sections into muffin tins, cut edges up. Bake 25 minutes.

Serving: 1 Roll	Calories: 108	Protein: 3 gm
Calories from Fat: 18	Total Fat: 2 gm	Dietary Fiber: 1 gm
Saturated Fat: 0 gm	Carbs: 19 gm	Sodium: 90 mg
Component of Fat: 17%	Cholesterol: 1 mg	Calcium: 28 mg

Sourdough Rye Twists

Real sourdough breads are made in stages over a period of many days.
These tasty treats are well worth the planning and preparation.

Sourdough:
$1/2$ cup rye flour
$1/4$ cup water
$1/2$ cake yeast, crumbled

Second Stage:
$3/4$ cup water
1 cup rye flour

Sponge:
$1^3/_4$ cups rye flour
$1^3/_4$ cups all-purpose flour
$1/2$ cake yeast, crumbled
1 cup water

Final Stage:
1 cup water
2 teaspoons salt
1 tablespoon caraway seed
$1^3/_4$ cups all-purpose flour

Kneading:
2 cups all-purpose flour

MAKES 2 DOZEN TWISTS

With a wooden spoon, combine sourdough ingredients in glass jar. Cover tightly. Keep in warm place 24 hours. Mix in second stage ingredients. Cover, and let rest 4 hours.

Pour sourdough into large non-aluminum bowl. With a wooden spoon, add sponge ingredients. Cover with a damp cloth, let rise in warm place until doubled in bulk. Add final stage ingredients. Mix until smooth, cover, and let rest 20 minutes. Turn onto kneading board and work in as much of the 2 cups of flour as needed to make a firm dough. Divide into halves until you have 48 balls of dough. Use your hands to roll each into a 5-inch length. Twist 2 lengths together, pinch ends and tuck underneath. Place on cookie sheet sprayed with non-stick oil. Allow to rise in warm place until doubled in bulk. Bake in preheated 350° oven 30 minutes.

Serving: 1 Twist	Calories: 151	Protein: 4 gm
Calories from Fat: 5	Total Fat: 1 gm	Dietary Fiber: 3 gm
Saturated Fat: 0 gm	Carbs: 32 gm	Sodium: 196 mg
Component of Fat: 3%	Cholesterol: 0 mg	Calcium: 10 mg

Hoecakes

This recipe is an adaptation of the original hoecakes the Indians taught the New England settlers to make.

1 cup stone-ground
   cornmeal
1/2 teaspoon salt
1 1/4 cups boiling water
2 tablespoons canola oil
1 1/2 cups milk

MAKES 2 DOZEN 4-INCH CAKES

Boil water in the bottom pan of a double boiler. In the top pan, heat the cornmeal and salt together. Stirring constantly, scald cornmeal by very slowly adding 1 1/4 cups boiling water. Continue stirring another 10 minutes, then add oil and milk. Remove from heat.

Heat griddle over medium-low heat, then spray with non-stick oil. Drop batter by the tablespoon onto hot griddle. Cook 10 minutes, or until golden brown. Flip and cook on second side. Serve with maple syrup and honey, or alongside a bowl of homemade soup.

Serving: 3 Cakes	Calories: 101	Protein: 3 gm
Calories from Fat: 36	Total Fat: 4 gm	Dietary Fiber: 1 gm
Saturated Fat: 0 gm	Carbs: 14 gm	Sodium: 175 mg
Component of Fat: 35%	Cholesterol: 1 mg	Calcium: 58 mg

Quick Sweet Wheat Bread

*This is a somewhat coarse bread that
goes very well with a summer garden or fruit salad.*

2$^1/_2$ cups whole-wheat
   flour
2 teaspoons double-acting
   baking powder
1 teaspoon baking soda
1 egg, beaten
$^1/_3$ cup molasses
$^1/_4$ cup brown sugar
3 tablespoons safflower oil
1$^1/_3$ cup non-fat plain
   yogurt or buttermilk

MAKES 9" x 5" LOAF

Preheat oven to 375°. Spray a 9" x 5" bread
pan with non-stick oil. Combine flour, baking
powder and baking soda. In a separate bowl,
mix egg, molasses, brown sugar and oil.

Add the flour blend alternately with yogurt or
buttermilk to the wet mixture. Pour into bread
pan. Bake about 50 minutes, or until loaf
sounds hollow when tapped on the bottom.

Serving: 1 Slice	Calories: 177	Protein: 5 gm
Calories from Fat: 38	Total Fat: 4.5 gm	Dietary Fiber: 3 gm
Saturated Fat: 1 gm	Carbs: 31 gm	Sodium: 216 mg
Component of Fat: 21%	Cholesterol: 18 mg	Calcium: 127 mg

Toasting White Bread

1 cup warm water
2 tablespoons sugar
1 pkg. active dry yeast
3 cups unbleached flour
$\frac{1}{4}$ teaspoon sea salt
$1\frac{1}{2}$ tablespoons unsalted
    butter, softened
4 teaspoons cornmeal
1 egg white

MAKES 1 LOAF

Combine water, sugar and yeast in a small bowl. Let stand 10 minutes. In a large mixing bowl, combine flour, salt, butter, and the yeast mixture. Knead 10 minutes. Spray another bowl with 3 coats of vegetable oil. Place dough in oiled bowl, turn to coat all sides. Cover bowl, set in warm place, and let rise until doubled in bulk.

Spray a 9" x 5" bread pan with non-stick oil. Dust pan with 2 teaspoons cornmeal. Punch down dough. Roll out into a 9" x 3" rectangle. Roll up rectangle into 9-inch long roll. Place in pan, seam down. Beat egg white and brush over top of loaf. Sprinkle with remaining cornmeal. Cover with plastic wrap, leaving extra room for expansion. Set in warm place, let rise until double in bulk. Bake in 400° oven 35 minutes.

Serving: 1 Slice	Calories: 148	Protein: 5 gm
Calories from Fat: 17	Total Fat: 2 gm	Dietary Fiber: 0 gm
Saturated Fat: 1 gm	Carbs: 29 gm	Sodium: 55 mg
Component of Fat: 11%	Cholesterol: 4 mg	Calcium: 7 mg

Herbed Buttermilk Bread

3$\frac{1}{2}$ cups low-fat
   buttermilk
2 pkgs. active dry yeast
1 teaspoon baking soda
1 teaspoon salt
$\frac{1}{4}$ cup sugar
1 tablespoon rosemary
1 tablespoon dill
1 teaspoon garlic powder
2 tablespoons melted
   butter
2 tablespoons canola oil
8 cups sifted all-purpose
   flour
canola oil for brushing
   tops of loaves

MAKES THREE 9" x 5" LOAVES

Heat buttermilk to 110°, then sprinkle yeast over top. Let rest 5 minutes, then stir to dissolve yeast. Add baking soda, sugar, herbs, butter and oil. Stir in as much flour as you can, then turn out onto board to knead in the rest.

Spray large bowl with vegetable oil. Place dough in bowl, and turn to coat all sides with oil. Cover, set in warm place, and let rise until doubled in bulk. Punch down and knead for 2 minutes. Divide dough into 3 parts and shape into loaves. Place in bread pans sprayed with non-stick oil. Brush tops with canola oil. Let rise until doubled in bulk. Bake in preheated 375° oven for 45 minutes.

Serving: 1 Slice
Calories from Fat: 23
Saturated Fat: 2 gm
Component of Fat: 14%

Calories: 127
Total Fat: 3 gm
Carbs: 24 gm
Cholesterol: 2 mg

Protein: 13 gm
Dietary Fiber: 1 gm
Sodium: 101 mg
Calcium: 35 mg

Oatmeal Bread

MAKES TWO 9" x 5" LOAVES

2 cups rolled oatmeal
$^1/_2$ teaspoon salt
3 cups boiling water
2 pkgs. active dry yeast
$^1/_4$ cup warm water
$^1/_2$ cup brown sugar
$^1/_2$ cup molasses
$2^1/_2$ tablespoons safflower oil
4 cups unbleached all-purpose flour
2 tablespoons each skim milk and rolled oats for tops of loaves

In a large mixing bowl, pour boiling water over oatmeal and salt. In a separate bowl, dissolve yeast in warm water, then mix into the oatmeal. Add brown sugar, molasses and oil. Blend well. Stir in as much flour as you can, then turn onto board to knead in the rest. Knead about 10 minutes or until dough is smooth and elastic.

Spray large bowl with 3 coats of vegetable oil. Place dough in bowl and turn to coat all sides. Cover and let rise in warm place until doubled in bulk. Punch down, and knead 2 minutes. Shape into two loaves and place in bread pans sprayed with non-stick oil. Brush tops of loaves with milk, then dust with rolled oats. Cover and let rise until doubled in bulk. Bake in preheated 375° oven 45 minutes, or until loaves sound hollow when tapped. Cool on a wire rack.

Serving: 1 Slice
Calories from Fat: 19
Saturated Fat: 0 gm
Component of Fat: 12%

Calories: 158
Total Fat: 2 gm
Carbs: 31 gm
Cholesterol: 0 mg

Protein: 4 gm
Dietary Fiber: 1 gm
Sodium: 53 mg
Calcium: 27 mg

Honey-Nut Picnic Brown Bread

1 cup sifted all-purpose
    flour
1 teaspoon baking soda
2 teaspoons baking powder
1 egg
2 cups graham flour
1$^1/_2$ cups low-fat
    buttermilk
$^1/_2$ cup honey
$^1/_2$ cup dark molasses
$^1/_4$ cup chopped walnuts

MAKES 9" x 5" LOAF

Preheat oven to 350°. Spray a 9" x 5" loaf pan with non-stick oil.

Sift together flour, baking soda and baking powder. Stir in remaining ingredients in the order listed.

Pour batter into pan and bake 1 hour, or until toothpick inserted in center comes out clean.

Serving: 1 Slice	Calories: 152	Protein: 15 gm
Calories from Fat: 32	Total Fat: 4 gm	Dietary Fiber: 0 gm
Saturated Fat: 2 gm	Carbs: 31 gm	Sodium: 222 mg
Component of Fat: 15%	Cholesterol: 18 mg	Calcium: 103 mg

The New England cookbooks and ladies' journals of the early and mid-nineteenth century clearly indicate a preference for flour and pastry products. Many cookbooks of the day contained at least 150 recipes for bread, yeast-making, rolls, biscuits, cakes and pastry. Most of this baking was done in a Dutch oven or over an open hearth fire.

Quick Apple-Cranberry Nut Bread

1 packed cup chopped
cranberries
$^1/_4$ cup sugar
6 tablespoons canola oil
1 cup light brown sugar
2 eggs
3 cups all-purpose flour
2 cups grated apples
3 tablespoons finely
chopped nuts
1 teaspoon baking soda
$1^1/_2$ tablespoons baking
powder
1 teaspoon lemon juice
1 tablespoon cinnamon
1 teaspoon nutmeg
$^1/_2$ teaspoon cloves
1 cup low-fat buttermilk

MAKES TWO 9" x 5" LOAVES

Preheat oven to 350°. Spray bread pans with non-stick oil.

Combine cranberries and sugar. In large mixing bowl, beat oil, sugar and eggs. In a third bowl, combine flour, apples, nuts, baking soda, baking powder, lemon juice and spices. Stir dry ingredients alternately with buttermilk into wet mixture. Fold in sugared cranberries. Pour batter into bread pans. Bake 1 hour or until toothpick inserted in center of loaves comes out clean. Wait 10 minutes before removing from pans, then cool on wire racks.

Serving: 1 Slice	Calories: 156	Protein: 3 gm
Calories from Fat: 32	Total Fat: 4 gm	Dietary Fiber: 1 gm
Saturated Fat: 0.5 gm	Carbs: 29 gm	Sodium: 151 mg
Component of Fat: 20%	Cholesterol: 18 mg	Calcium: 61 mg

Cinnamon-Pecan Bread

1 cup skim milk
1 cup lukewarm water
2 tablespoons canola oil
$^1/_3$ cup packed brown
    sugar
1 teaspoon salt
1 pkg. active dry yeast
$^1/_4$ cup 110° water
$6^1/_2$ cups sifted all-
    purpose flour
2 tablespoons melted
    unsalted butter
$^1/_2$ cup sugar
2 tablespoons cinnamon
$^1/_2$ cup chopped pecans

For tops of loaves:
2 tablespoons milk
2 tablespoons sugar
2 teaspoons cinnamon

MAKES 2 LOAVES

Scald milk. In a large mixing bowl, combine milk water, oil, brown sugar and salt. In a separate bowl, sprinkle yeast over warm water. Let sit 5 minutes, stir until yeast dissolves, then pour into milk mixture. Mix in 3 cups of flour, then turn onto board and knead in remaining flour. Knead 10 minutes or until smooth and elastic. Spray mixing bowl with oil, and turn dough in bowl to coat all sides. Cover and let rise in warm place until doubled in bulk.

Punch down dough and roll into two 9" x 14" rectangles. Brush with melted butter, sprinkle with sugar, cinnamon and pecans. Roll up jelly-roll fashion into 9-inch lengths, then place seam side down in pans sprayed with non-stick oil. Brush tops with milk, sprinkle with cinnamon and sugar. Let rise until doubled in bulk. Bake in 350° oven 45 minutes.

Serving: 1 Slice
Calories from Fat: 37
Saturated Fat: 1 gm
Component of Fat: 18%

Calories: 196
Total Fat: 4 gm
Carbs: 36 gm
Cholesterol: 3 mg

Protein: 4 gm
Dietary Fiber: 2 gm
Sodium: 106 mg
Calcium: 33 mg

Appetizers
and
Finger Food

CONTENTS

Appetizers can be used as a main dish by doubling the amount of food per serving.

Carrot-Cheese Quiche Tarts

Tart Shells:
1½ cups plain non-fat
cracker crumbs
1½ tablespoons canola oil
3 tablespoons skim milk

Filling:
1 cup grated carrots
1 teaspoon canola oil
2 eggs, beaten
1 cup non-fat sour cream
1 teaspoon Worcestershire
sauce
1 cup grated low-fat
Swiss Lorraine cheese

MAKES 6 TARTS

Preheat oven to 375°. Spray six 3-inch tart shells (or a 9-inch pie plate) with non-stick oil. Put crushed cracker crumbs in a mixing bowl. Sprinkle with oil and milk. Distribute moisture throughout with a pastry cutter or fork. Press crumbs into tart shells and work up the sides. Bake 5 minutes.

Sauté carrots in oil over medium-high heat for 5 minutes. Drain off liquid. In a medium-sized mixing bowl, beat eggs, sour cream and Worcestershire sauce. Stir in cheese and carrots. Pour into tart shells. Bake 30 minutes or until golden brown.

Serving: 1 Tart
Calories from Fat: 60
Saturated Fat: 1.5 gm
Component of Fat: 24%

Calories: 250
Total Fat: 7 gm
Carbs: 34 gm
Cholesterol: 78 mg

Protein: 13 gm
Dietary Fiber: 2 gm
Sodium: 122 mg
Calcium: 258 mg

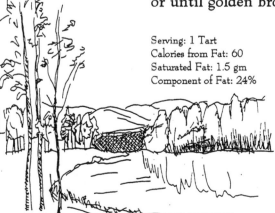

Deviled Shrimp

12 medium-large eggs
$^1/_2$ cup non-fat mayonnaise
2 tablespoons lemon juice
$^1/_2$ teaspoon chopped
    fresh dill
$^1/_2$ teaspoon horseradish
$^1/_2$ teaspoon black pepper
$^1/_2$ lb. small bay shrimp
1 tablespoon paprika

SERVES 12

Hard-boil eggs (about 7 minutes in boiling water.) Peel and slice eggs in half lengthwise. Remove yolks, reserving yolks of 4 eggs, and discarding the other 8 yolks.

Mash together the 4 yolks, mayonnaise, lemon juice, dill, horseradish and black pepper. Fold in bay shrimp.   Fill egg white halves with mixture. Sprinkle with paprika, and arrange on platter with parsley or lettuce garnish.

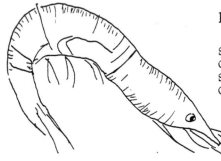

Serving: 1/12 Recipe
Calories from Fat: 17
Saturated Fat: 1 gm
Component of Fat: 29%

Calories: 64
Total Fat: 2 gm
Carbs: 3 gm
Cholesterol: 100 mg

Protein: 8 gm
Dietary Fiber: 0 gm
Sodium: 157 mg
Calcium: 20 mg

Most egg laying hens on nineteenth century New England farms roamed free. They did not lay as many eggs as hens do today, because modern hen feed includes egg-inducing vitamins and nutrients. Only the wealthiest New England farmers with a large number of hens could afford to have a dozen eggs served at one meal.

Broiled Scallop Hors d'Oeuvres

1 lb. scallops
1 pint cherry tomatoes
$^1/_2$ cup safflower oil
4 tablespoons vinegar
1 tablespoon tamari or
    soy sauce
1 teaspoon basil
1 teaspoon pepper
1 teaspoon garlic powder

SERVES 6

Wash scallops and cherry tomatoes. In a wide, shallow bowl, mix remaining ingredients to make marinade. Add scallops and tomatoes. Refrigerator at least two hours, stirring occasionally. Alternate scallops and tomatoes on skewers. Reserve marinade for basting.

Outdoor grilling: Remove grill from flames, and spray with non-stick oil. Place skewers on grill. Depending on heat of coals and size of scallops, cook 8-12 minutes, turning and basting every 2-3 minutes. Broiling: Preheat broiler. Rest end of skewers on sides of an oven pan, and set on upper rack. Broil 10-12 minutes, turning and basting as needed.

Serving: 1/6 Recipe	Calories: 108	Protein: 14 gm
Calories from Fat: 28	Total Fat: 3 gm	Dietary Fiber: 1 gm
Saturated Fat: 0.5 gm	Carbs: 7 gm	Sodium: 300 mg
Component of Fat: 25%	Cholesterol: 25 mg	Calcium: 29 mg

Vegetable Strudel

Filling:

SERVES 12

2 large onions, chopped
2 cloves minced garlic
3 stalks celery
1 tablespoon canola oil
3 large carrots, peeled
1 lb. asparagus
2 red peppers
2 cups cooked spinach
1 tablespoon pepper
$1/4$ cup grated Gruyere cheese
2 tablespoons chopped walnuts
$1/2$ cup plain bread crumbs

Pastry Dough:

2 cups flour
$1/8$ teaspoon baking soda
2 eggs
2 tablespoons canola oil
1 teaspoon vinegar
2 tablespoons water

Brushing:

2 teaspoons canola oil
1 teaspoon paprika

In a large saucepan, sauté onions, garlic and celery in oil. Chop carrots, asparagus and peppers, add to pan and stir-fry 5 minutes. Press liquid from cooked spinach. In a mixing bowl, combine all filling ingredients, cover, and refrigerate at least 2 hours.

Combine pastry dough ingredients in a mixer, then cover to prevent drying out. On a floured cloth, roll out dough very thin. Cut into nine 9" x 12" rectangles. Lightly brush rectangles with oil. Spray 9" x 12" oven pan with non-stick oil. Place 3 layers of pastry dough in pan, cover with half the filling. Layer 3 more sheets of dough, and cover with remaining filling. Place final 3 sheets of dough on top. Brush top with oil and spinkle paprika. Use a sharp knife to mark cutting lines in top pastry layer. Bake in 350° oven 25 minutes. Cool in pan 2 minutes, and serve hot.

Serving: 1/12 Recipe	Calories: 204	Protein: 8 gm
Calories from Fat: 66	Total Fat: 7 gm	Dietary Fiber: 4 gm
Saturated Fat: 1 gm	Carbs: 28 gm	Sodium: 120 mg
Component of Fat: 31%	Cholesterol: 38 mg	Calcium: 112 mg

Smoked Salmon Toasts

$^1/_2$ lb. smoked salmon
1 tablespoon vermouth
1 scallion, chopped fine
1 egg whites, beaten
2 tablespoons sesame
    seeds
$^1/_2$ teaspoon minced garlic
1 teaspoon cornstarch
8 slices white bread
4 teaspoons canola oil for
    frying

SERVES 8

Cut smoked salmon into small pieces. Mix with vermouth, scallion, egg whites, sesame seeds, garlic and cornstarch. Let rest 15 minutes.

Spray a large frying pan with non-stick oil. Pour 2 teaspoons canola oil into pan, preheat oil on medium-high.

Trim crust from bread, then cut each piece into four triangles. Cover each triangle with 1 tablespoon salmon mixture. Fry 16 toast pieces, salmon side down, until golden brown. Remove with slotted spatula and drain on paper towels. Repeat frying process for remaining toasts.

Serving: 1/8 Recipe	Calories: 143	Protein: 9 gm
Calories from Fat: 50	Total Fat: 6 gm	Dietary Fiber: 1 gm
Saturated Fat: 1 gm	Carbs: 14 gm	Sodium: 370 mg
Component of Fat: 35%	Cholesterol: 7 mg	Calcium: 54 mg

Almond Crab Pâté

16 oz. fresh crab meat
2 eggs, separated
½ cup skimmed
   evaporated milk
1 small onion, grated
2 teaspoons soft butter
2 tablespoons brandy
1 tablespoon port wine
½ teaspoon saffron
2 tablespoons almond
   slivers
2 tablespoons flour
salt to taste
½ teaspoon white pepper

SERVES 6

Preheat oven to 325°, and set kettle of water to boil. Divide crab meat into 3 parts. Put the first part in the blender with egg yolks, process until smooth. Mix the second part with milk. Mix the third part with remaining ingredients (except the egg whites). Whip egg whites until stiff. Lightly combine egg whites with the 3 crab meat mixtures. Spray small ceramic dish with non-stick oil. Pour into dish and cover tightly with aluminum foil. Set pâté dish into larger baking dish. Pour boiling water into larger baking dish, half the height of pâté dish. Bake 1-1½ hours, or until set. Chill, and serve with low-fat plain or rice crackers.

Serving: 1/6 Recipe	Calories: 174	Protein: 18 gm
Calories from Fat: 55	Total Fat: 6 gm	Dietary Fiber: 1 gm
Saturated Fat: 2 gm	Carbs: 8 gm	Sodium: 458 mg
Component of Fat: 32%	Cholesterol: 152 mg	Calcium: 114 mg

Marvelous Greek Mushrooms

1 lb. fresh mushrooms
(small if possible)
2 cups vegetable bouillon
broth (from cubes)
$^1/_4$ cup lemon juice

Tie in a cheesecloth:
12 peppercorns
4" stalk of celery
4 springs parsley
2 cloves garlic
sprig of fresh, or a pinch
of dried, thyme
6 coriander seeds

SERVES 4

Wash and trim stem end of mushrooms. If mushrooms are large, cut in quarters, if medium-sized, cut in half.

Combine broth, lemon juice and spice bag in a pot, bring to a boil. Add mushrooms and stir. Cover pot, reduce heat and simmer 10 minutes. Remove mushrooms with a slotted spoon, and arrange in a serving dish. Rapidly boil down the liquid until it is reduced to about $^3/_4$-cup. Remove spice bag. Adjust seasonings. Strain liquid over mushrooms. Serve hot or cold.

Serving: 1/4 Recipe	Calories: 5	Protein: 11 gm
Calories from Fat:	Total Fat: 0 gm	Dietary Fiber: 3 gm
Saturated Fat: 0 gm	Carbs: 2 gm	Sodium: 1 mg
Component of Fat: 21%	Cholesterol: 0 mg	Calcium: 22 mg

Chatham Haddock Balls

1½ lbs. haddock, fresh
   or frozen
6 medium potatoes,
   baked and scooped
   out of the skins
2 eggs
3 tablespoons skim milk
2 tablespoons grated onion
2 tablespoons grated
   Parmesan cheese
1 tablespoon lemon juice
salt and pepper to taste
¼ cup canola oil for frying
½ cup skim milk for
   dipping
¼ cup flour for dipping

SERVES 10

Drain haddock and pat dry. Put haddock through meat grinder or chop into very small pieces. Rice or mash potatoes, then mix with fish. Beat in eggs, then blend in milk, onion, cheese, lemon juice and spices. Roll into 1-inch balls. Spray frying pan with non-stick oil. Pour canola oil into pan, and preheat over medium-high burner for 7 minutes.

Dip haddock balls in milk, then roll in flour. Fry in hot pan until light brown. Serve with seafood or tartare sauce.

Serving: 1/10 Recipe
Calories from Fat: 66
Saturated Fat: 1 gm
Component of Fat: 34%

Calories: 194
Total Fat: 7 gm
Carbs: 14 gm
Cholesterol: 83 mg

Protein: 17 gm
Dietary Fiber: 1 gm
Sodium: 100 mg
Calcium: 68 mg

Garden Style Antipasto

4 large fresh tomatoes
2 peppers, different colors
1 cup julienned carrots
2 celery stalks, sliced
2 oz. part-skim
      mozzarella cheese
8 pitted Italian olives
1 tablespoon olive oil
1 tablespoon lime juice
2 tablespoons wine
      vinegar
3 tablespoons white wine
1 tablespoon fresh
      summer savory
3 tablespoons fresh
      chopped parsley
1 tablespoon fresh
      chopped basil
salt and pepper to taste

SERVES 4

Slice tomatoes into thick rounds.   Arrange tomato slices together on each salad plate.   Slice peppers into strips, mix together strips of both color peppers,   and place next to tomatoes. Place julienned carrots and sliced celery next to each other on the plates. Slice mozzarella into wedges and place between tomatoes and celery. Place 2 black olives in the middle of each plate.

Combine remaining ingredients in a jar. Shake well at least 3 minutes. Sprinkle over vegetables and mozzarella. Chill antipasto plates before serving.

Serving: 1/4 Recipe	Calories: 161	Protein: 6 gm
Calories from Fat: 73	Total Fat: 8 gm	Dietary Fiber: 5 gm
Saturated Fat: 2.5 gm	Carbs: 17 gm	Sodium: 278 mg
Component of Fat: 42%	Cholesterol: 10 mg	Calcium: 157 mg

4th of July Cherry Bombs

1 pint cherry tomatoes
$\frac{1}{2}$ cup low-fat cream
    cheese, softened
1 teaspoon finely grated
    onion
1 tablespoon fresh
    chopped cilantro
1 teaspoon cumin
$\frac{1}{2}$ teaspoon black pepper
pinch of cayenne
pinch of salt
$\frac{1}{2}$ cup small cooked bay
    shrimp
paprika for garnishing

SERVES 6

With a sharp knife, cut tops off cherry tomatoes. Use a small serated grapefruit teaspoon to scoop out pulp. Put pulp in a small mixing bowl with cream cheese. With a fork, mash and blend cream cheese and pulp, and mix in spices.

Drain shrimp and pat dry in paper towels. Chop into small pieces, then gently stir into cream cheese mixture. Place in pastry bag, and squeeze to fill cherry tomatoes. Sprinkle tops with paprika.

Serving: 1/6 Recipe	Calories: 57	Protein: 8 gm
Calories from Fat: 7	Total Fat: 1 gm	Dietary Fiber: 1 gm
Saturated Fat: 0 gm	Carbs: 4 gm	Sodium: 160 mg
Component of Fat: 13%	Cholesterol: 49 mg	Calcium: 30 mg

Although the Declaration of Independence was signed July 4, 1776, the British sent fighting ships to "take back" the colonies. From 1775 to 1815, war raged over the seas of coastal New England for 29 of these years. With much of the war-time demands falling on Boston and New York, smaller cities took on a greater domestic importance. (cont.)

Cucumber Finger Teas

These nifty little tea sandwiches
are a light lunchtime favorite on hot summer days.

$^1/_3$ cup low-fat
    mayonnaise
$^1/_2$ teaspoon lemon juice
pinch of dill
pinch of pepper
pinch of salt
1 large cold cucumber
8 slices sourdough bread

SERVES 4

Combine mayonnaise, lemon juice and spices in small mixing bowl. Adjust seasonings to taste. Peel cucumber and slice into very thin rounds. Cut some rounds in half.

Trim crust from bread. With a rolling pin, lightly roll bread slices, compacting to half their original thickness. Spread seasoned mayonnaise on a slice of bread, cover with 2 layers of cucumbers, placing half-rounds along edges, and cover with another slice of rolled bread. Cut sandwiches diagonally.

Serving: 1 Sandwich	Calories: 180	Protein: 5 gm
Calories from Fat: 26	Total Fat: 3 gm	Dietary Fiber: 2 gm
Saturated Fat: 0.5 gm	Carbs: 33 gm	Sodium: 519 mg
Component of Fat: 15%	Cholesterol: 0 mg	Calcium: 48 mg

(cont.) Around the turn of the nineteenth century, many small fishing villages developed into economic centers of commerce, education, culture, and support services for war-time needs. Among the new thriving cities were Newport (one of the young nations' major ports of the 1800's), New London, Portsmouth, and Portland.

Crazy Crab Dip

SERVES 8

1 lb. fresh crabmeat
1 cup non-fat sour cream
8 oz. non-fat cream
cheese, softened at
room temperature
2 teaspoons finely
chopped scallion
1 tablespoon lemon juice
2 teaspoons dry sherry
dash hot pepper sauce
salt and pepper to taste
1/2 cup chopped water
chestnuts
1 teaspoon paprika

Preheat oven to 350°. Clean crab meat, checking for shell pieces.

With a whisk, whip together sour cream, cream cheese, scallion, lemon juice, sherry, hot pepper sauce, salt and pepper. Stir in chopped water chestnuts, then crab meat. Place in ovenproof serving dish. Sprinkle with paprika. Bake 30 minutes, or until bubbly. Serve this zesty dip hot or cold, with toast points or crackers for dipping.

Serving: 1/8 Recipe   Calories: 130   Protein: 16 gm
Calories from Fat: 16   Total Fat: 2 gm   Dietary Fiber: 0 gm
Saturated Fat: 0.5 gm   Carbs: 10 gm   Sodium: 479 mg
Component of Fat: 13%   Cholesterol: 59 mg   Calcium: 120 mg

Pesto Guacamole Dip

Serve with white or blue corn baked chips for a fabulous treat!

¹/₂ cup non-fat plain
    yogurt
¹/₂ cup non-fat cottage
    cheese
2 cloves crushed garlic
¹/₂ cup packed fresh basil
    leaves
¹/₂ tablespoon olive oil
1 tablespoon grated onion
8 drops hot pepper sauce
1 tablespoon Parmesan
1 tablespoon pine nuts
2 medium sized avocados
1 tablespoons lemon juice
1¹/₂ cups finely chopped
    tomatoes
salt and pepper to taste

MAKES 4 CUPS

In a blender, whip together yogurt and cottage cheese until smooth. With blender running on high speed, drop in crushed garlic, basil leaves, olive oil, onion, hot pepper sauce, Parmesan cheese and pine nuts. Blend until smooth.   In a mixing bowl, mash avacado and sprinkle with lemon juice. Fold blender mixture into avocado, then add chopped tomatoes, salt and pepper.

Serving: 1/4 Cup	Calories: 66	Protein: 2 gm
Calories from Fat: 39	Total Fat: 4 gm	Dietary Fiber: 3 gm
Saturated Fat: 1 gm	Carbs: 6 gm	Sodium: 51 mg
Component of Fat: 55%	Cholesterol: 1 mg	Calcium: 30 mg

Apricot Fruit Dip

2 cups dried apricots
4 cup orange juice
$^1/_2$ cup unsweetened
    applesauce
4 tablespoons honey
$^1/_2$ teaspoon cinnamon
$^1/_2$ teaspoon nutmeg
2 teaspoons vanilla extract

MAKES 3 CUPS

Chop dried apricots into small pieces. Place in glass or ceramic saucepan with orange juice. Using a wooden spoon (never aluminum), stir and mash apricots as the mixture is brought to a boil. Reduce heat, and simmer until all liquid is absorbed. Remove from stove.

Mix in applesauce, honey, cinnamon and nutmeg and vanilla. Cover, and chill at least 2 hours before serving. This dip is wonderful with fresh summer fruits.

Serving: 1/4 Cup	Calories: 118	Protein: 1 gm
Calories from Fat: 2	Total Fat: 0 gm	Dietary Fiber: 2 gm
Saturated Fat: 0 gm	Carbs: 30 gm	Sodium: 4 mg
Component of Fat: 1%	Cholesterol: 0 mg	Calcium: 19 mg

Salads
and
Fresh Greens

CONTENTS

Apple-Raisin Cole Slaw

$^1/_3$ cup low-fat cottage
   cheese

$^1/_3$ cup non-fat plain yogurt

2 tablespoons low-fat
   mayonnaise

1 tablespoon sugar

1 teaspoon pepper

pinch of salt

3 grated McIntosh apples

3 grated Granny Smith
   apples

$^1/_2$ cup golden raisins

1 tablespoon lemon juice

3 cups grated cabbage

SERVES 6

Combine cottage cheese, yogurt, mayonnaise, sugar, pepper and salt in blender. Whip until smooth.

In a large mixing bowl, sprinkle lemon juice over grated apples and raisins, and toss. Add cabbage. Mix in dressing. Serve immediately, or cover and chill.

Serving: 1/6 Recipe	Calories: 174	Protein: 4 gm
Calories from Fat: 22	Total Fat: 2.5 gm	Dietary Fiber: 5 gm
Saturated Fat: 1 gm	Carbs: 38 gm	Sodium: 124 mg
Component of Fat: 12%	Cholesterol: 1 mg	Calcium: 65 mg

Marinated Lentil Salad

SERVES 6

3 cups boiling water
1 cup dried lentils
1 peeled onion stuck with
    3 cloves
1 bay leaf
1 clove garlic, minced
1 teaspoon oregano
2 tablespoons olive oil
3 tablespoons wine
    vinegar
1 cup chopped peeled
    tomatoes, drained
2 tablespoons finely
    chopped chives
salt and pepper to taste

Simmer lentils in boiling water with onion, cloves, bay leaf and garlic. When lentils are tender, in about 45 minutes, drain. Discard onion, bay leaf and garlic.

Add oregano, olive oil and vinegar to lentils. Mix in tomatoes, chives, salt and pepper. Chill before serving.

Serving: 1/6 Recipe	Calories: 161	Protein: 9 gm
Calories from Fat: 44	Total Fat: 5 gm	Dietary Fiber: 10 gm
Saturated Fat: 1 gm	Carbs: 20 gm	Sodium: 100 mg
Component of Fat: 27%	Cholesterol: 0 mg	Calcium: 32 mg

Block Island, Rhode Island, has been rated one of the 12 best unspoiled areas in the Western Hemisphere. Southeast Light on Mohegan Bluffs is one of its spectacular overlooks. Accessible by ferry, Block Island offers scenic trails, bike paths, wildlife sanctuaries and even guided horseback tours across meadows and shorelands.

Egg and Potato Salad

3 lbs. potatoes (about 9 medium-sized spuds)

4 eggs

2 tablespoons safflower oil

2 tablespoons lemon juice

$1/2$ small onion, grated

1 teaspoon dill

1 teaspoon Tabasco sauce

1 cup celery, chopped fine

$1/3$ cup non-fat mayonnaise

$1/3$ cup non-fat sour cream

3 tablespoons low-fat buttermilk

$1/2$ teaspoon salt

1 teaspoon pepper

SERVES 8

Peel potatoes. Dice into bite-sized pieces and boil until tender. While potatoes are cooking, add eggs to boiling water and hard-boil (about 6 minutes). Remove eggs with slotted spoon, set in cold water, when cool enough to handle, remove shells. Chop eggs and set aside. When potatoes are cooked, drain and chill.

In a small mixing bowl, combine remaining ingredients, cover and chill. When potatoes are cold, mix with chopped egg and dressing.

Serving: 1/8 Recipe	Calories: 215	Protein: 8 gm
Calories from Fat: 54	Total Fat: 6 gm	Dietary Fiber: 4 gm
Saturated Fat: 1 gm	Carbs: 32 gm	Sodium: 300 mg
Component of Fat: 25%	Cholesterol: 108 mg	Calcium: 59 mg

Rainbow Pepper-Pasta Salad

1 lb. tri-colored pasta
    spirals
1 medium-sized onion
4 peppers of assorted
    colors (red, yellow,
    purple, orange, green)
2 tablespoons safflower oil
$^1/_3$ cup herbed vinegar
1 clove garlic, minced
$^1/_2$ teaspoon oregano
$^1/_2$ teaspoon basil
$^1/_2$ teaspoon dill
4 tablespoons diced
    pimento
$^1/_2$ cup non-fat mayonnaise
2 teaspoons lemon juice
salt and pepper to taste

SERVES 6

Boil pasta until tender, drain. Transfer to a large bowl, cover and chill.

Cut onion and peppers into thin slices. Heat safflower oil in large skillet. Stir-fry onion and peppers, just until onions are beginning to clear. Add vegetables to pasta.

Combine remaining ingredients to make dressing, mix well. Pour over pasta and peppers, toss gently. Chill before serving.

Serving: 1/6 Recipe
Calories from Fat: 50
Saturated Fat: 1 gm
Component of Fat: 13%

Calories: 358
Total Fat: 6 gm
Carbs: 66 gm
Cholesterol: 0 mg

Protein: 11 gm
Dietary Fiber: 2 gm
Sodium: 194 mg
Calcium: 45 mg

Creamy Beets

6 medium-sized beets
$^2/_3$ cup non-fat plain
    yogurt
1 tablespoon cider vinegar
1 tablespoon chopped
    parsley
1 teaspoon chopped chives
salt and pepper to taste

SERVES 4

Scrub beets and cut off ends. Simmer in boiling water 40 minutes, or until tender. When cool enough to handle, peel and slice.

In a small bowl, combine remaining ingredients. Mix beets with yogurt sauce. Serve cold, or warm briefly before serving.

Serving: 1/4 Recipe	Calories: 55	Protein: 3 gm
Calories from Fat: 2	Total Fat: 0 gm	Dietary Fiber: 1 gm
Saturated Fat: 0 gm	Carbs: 11 gm	Sodium: 117 mg
Component of Fat: 3%	Cholesterol: 1 mg	Calcium: 84 mg

Robust Romaine Salad

The beautiful and peppery nasturtium blooms dress up this lively salad.
(Be sure to use flowers that have not been chemically sprayed.)

2 heads romaine lettuce
28 fresh nasturtium
    flowers in assorted
    colors
$^1/_2$ cup peeled and grated
    carrot
2 tablespoons fresh basil,
    parsley and/or dill

SERVES 6

Wash, dry and tear romaine. Combine romaine with nasturtiums, grated carrot and herb.

Serve with choice of salad dressing. Raspberry-Lime Vinaigrette is superb on this salad.

Suggested dressings for this salad are:
Raspberry-Lime Vinaigrette, page 63
Creamy Dill Dressing, page 64

Serving: 1/6 Recipe
Calories from Fat: 5
Saturated Fat: 0 gm
Component of Fat: 9%

Calories: 46
Total Fat: 1 gm
Carbs: 7 gm
Cholesterol: 0 mg

Protein: 4 gm
Dietary Fiber: 6 gm
Sodium: 25 mg
Calcium: 90 mg

There are many edible flowers that can be tossed in salads. In addition to the peppery taste of nasturtiums, try these other flowers for color, flavor, and scent: cottage pinks and carnations, pansies, tulips, lilac, blue borage, rose petals, chive flowers, marigolds and hollyhock blossoms. Flowers can be poisonous, so use only those you are sure of.

Garden Tomato Marinate

4 large beefsteak-type
    tomatoes
1 large sweet onion,
    Vidalia or red
1 long cucumber

Dressing:
$1^1/_2$ tablespoons canola oil
$^1/_2$ cup balsamic vinegar
$^1/_4$ cup white wine
1 tablespoon sugar
1 tablespoon finely
    minced shallot
1 teaspoon garlic, minced
1 teaspoon Dijon mustard
2 tablespoons parsley
salt and pepper to taste

SERVES 4

Slice tomatoes into thick rounds. Peel and cut onion into very thin rings. Peel cucumber and slice into rounds. Place vegetables in shallow bowl.

In glass jar with tight-fitting lid, shake well to combine ingredients for dressing. Adjust seasonings to taste. Pour over vegetables, toss, cover, and chill at least 2 hours.

Serving: 1/4 Recipe	Calories: 163	Protein: 2 gm
Calories from Fat: 52	Total Fat: 6 gm	Dietary Fiber: 3 gm
Saturated Fat: 0.5 gm	Carbs: 24 gm	Sodium: 59 mg
Component of Fat: 31%	Cholesterol: 0 mg	Calcium: 40 mg

Chicory & Endive Salad

2 tablespoons olive oil
1 clove garlic, halved
2 tablespoons lemon juice
2 tablespoons white wine
    vinegar
$^1/_2$ cup vegetable broth
salt and pepper to taste
6 packed cups chicory
    (curly endive) leaves
3 Belgian endives
$^1/_4$ cup (1 oz.) crumbled
    Roquefort cheese

SERVES 6

In a glass jar, mix olive oil, garlic clove halves, lemon juice, vinegar, broth, salt and pepper. Shake well. Chill in refrigerator at least 2 hours, then discard garlic.

Wash, dry and tear chicory leaves. Cut off base end of Belgian endives, then half crosswise and cut lengthwise into thin strips. Combine leaves in salad bowl.

Crumble Roquefort cheese over salad. Pour on dressing, and toss.

Serving: 1/6 Recipe	Calories: 110	Protein: 5 gm
Calories from Fat: 59	Total Fat: 7 gm	Dietary Fiber: 8 gm
Saturated Fat: 2 gm	Carbs: 11 gm	Sodium: 200 mg
Component of Fat: 49%	Cholesterol: 4 mg	Calcium: 226 mg

Asparagus and Pine Nut Salad

1 lb. fresh asparagus
1 clove garlic
3 tablespoons diced
      pimento
1 tablespoon fresh dill
4 teaspoons pine nuts,
      coarsely chopped
1 tablespoon olive oil
2 tablespoons balsamic
      vinegar
1 teaspoon lemon juice
salt and pepper to taste

SERVES 4

Cut off base ends of asparagus, discard. Cut asparagus into $1/2$-inch pieces and briefly steam just until tender. Drain and chill.

Cut garlic clove in half and rub on inside of wooden salad bowl, then discard. Toss chilled asparagus pieces with remaining ingredients. Chill well and toss, again, before serving.

Serving: 1/4 Recipe	Calories: 87	Protein: 4 gm
Calories from Fat: 52	Total Fat: 6 gm	Dietary Fiber: 1 gm
Saturated Fat: 1 gm	Carbs: 5 gm	Sodium: 66 mg
Component of Fat: 58%	Cholesterol: 0 mg	Calcium: 19 mg

Maine Shrimp Salad

1 lb. small cooked shrimp,
  shelled and deveined
$\frac{1}{3}$ cup non-fat cottage
  cheese
$\frac{1}{3}$ cup non-fat plain
  yogurt
$\frac{1}{4}$ cup low-fat buttermilk
1 teaspoon lemon juice
2 tablespoons chopped dill
2 teaspoons prepared
  horseradish sauce
1 teaspoon black pepper
2 cups peeled, seeded and
  diced cucumber

SERVES 5

Chill shrimp in covered bowl. Combine remaining ingredients in blender and process until smooth. Mix into chilled shrimp, cover and chill at least 2 hours more.

Serving: 1/5 Recipe
Calories from Fat: 15
Saturated Fat: 1 gm
Component of Fat: 12%

Calories: 125
Total Fat: 2 gm
Carbs: 4 gm
Cholesterol: 180 mg

Protein: 23 gm
Dietary Fiber: 0 gm
Sodium: 300 mg
Calcium: 97 mg

Portland Head Light
Fort Williams Park
Cape Elizabeth, Maine

New England towns have been under the jurisdiction of many countries. In 1604 Samuel de Champlain, explorer of King Henry IV of France, came ashore in Castine, Maine. Castine has since existed under the flags of France, Britain, Holland and the United States. Many small coastal towns have a colorful history worth exploring.

Tomato-Olive Aspic

2 tablespoons gelatin
1/4 cup cold water
1/2 cup boiling vegetable
    bouillon broth
2 cups low-sodium tomato
    juice
2 tablespoons vinegar
1 tablespoon lemon juice
1 teaspoon paprika
1 teaspoon tarragon
1/2 teaspoon celery salt
1/2 teaspoon white pepper
pinch of sugar
1/4 cup chopped olives
1/4 cup chopped celery
1/2 cup minced pimento

SERVES 8

Soak gelatin in cold water. Add boiling bouillon broth and stir until gelatin is dissolved. Add tomato juice, vinegar, lemon juice, spices and sugar. Allow to thicken at room temperature.

Pour into mold and chill. When almost ready to set, sprinkle olives, celery and pimento over aspic, and lightly stir. Chill until firm.

To unmold: Briefly set lower part of mold in warm water. Turn out onto platter.

Serving: 1/8 Recipe	Calories: 37	Protein: 3 gm
Calories from Fat: 7	Total Fat: 1 gm	Dietary Fiber: 1 gm
Saturated Fat: 0 gm	Carbs: 5 gm	Sodium: 218 mg
Component of Fat: 19%	Cholesterol: 0 mg	Calcium: 24 mg

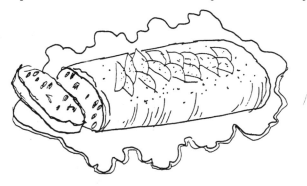

Orange-Beet Salad

8 medium-sized beets
1 pkg. orange-flavored
   gelatin
1 cup boiling water
$^3/_4$ cup beet juice
2 tablespoons vinegar
1 tablespoon finely grated
   onion
1 tablespoon prepared
   horseradish
$^3/_4$ cup celery, chopped
   fine

SERVES 8

Boil whole fresh beets in 3 cups water until tender.   Remove beets with slotted spoon, reserving $^3/_4$ cup beet juice. When cool enough to handle, peel skins from beets and dice into small pieces.

Dissolve gelatin in 1 cup boiling water. Mix in beet juice, vinegar, onion and horseradish. Pour into wet mold. Chill.

Just before jelly sets, stir in beets and celery. Refrigerate until firm, about 4 hours more.

Serving: 1/8 Recipe	Calories: 94	Protein: 2 gm
Calories from Fat: 14	Total Fat: 1.5 gm	Dietary Fiber: 1 gm
Saturated Fat: .5 gm	Carbs: 20 gm	Sodium: 89 mg
Component of Fat: 14%	Cholesterol: 1 mg	Calcium: 19 mg

Raspberry-Lime Vinaigrette

$1/3$ cup puréed raspberries
3 tablespoons lime juice
2 tablespoons sugar
$1/4$ cup dry white wine
$1/4$ cup red wine vinegar
2 tablespoons parsley
1 clove garlic, minced
salt and pepper to taste

MAKES 1 CUP

Combine all ingredients in glass jar with tight-fitting lid. Shake well. Chill before serving.

Serving: 2 Tablespoons	Calories: 26	Protein: 0 gm
Calories from Fat: 1	Total Fat: 0 gm	Dietary Fiber: 1 gm
Saturated Fat: 0 gm	Carbs: 5 gm	Sodium: 17 mg
Component of Fat: 2%	Cholesterol: 0 mg	Calcium: 8 mg

Honey French Dressing

$1/4$ cup low-sodium ketchup
2 tablespoons olive oil
2 tablespoons safflower oil
2 tablespoons lemon juice
2 tablespoons wine vinegar
$1/4$ cup honey
salt, pepper and Tabasco
    sauce to taste

MAKES $1^1/4$ CUPS

With all ingredients at room temperature, combine in a glass jar with tight-fitting lid. Shake well to blend. Chill. Shake before using.

Serving: 2 Tablespoons	Calories: 83	Protein: 0 gm
Calories from Fat: 36	Total Fat: 4 gm	Dietary Fiber: 0 gm
Saturated Fat: 1 gm	Carbs: 13 gm	Sodium: 69 mg
Component of Fat: 41%	Cholesterol: 0 mg	Calcium: 1 mg

Creamy Dill Dressing

$^1/_2$ cup non-fat mayonnaise
$^3/_4$ cup non-fat plain
    yogurt
1 clove garlic, pressed
1 teaspoon Worcestershire
    sauce
1 tablespoon fresh dill
1 teaspoon chervil
1 teaspoon parsley

MAKES $1^1/_4$ CUPS

Blend all ingredients together. Chill well before serving.

Serving: 2 Tablespoons	Calories: 18	Protein: 1 gm
Calories from Fat: 0	Total Fat: 0 gm	Dietary Fiber: 0 gm
Saturated Fat: 0 gm	Carbs: 3 gm	Sodium: 102 mg
Component of Fat: 1%	Cholesterol: 0 mg	Calcium: 33 mg

Russian Dressing

$^1/_2$ cup non-fat mayonnaise
$^1/_2$ cup non-fat sour cream
1 tablespoon prepared
    horseradish
$^1/_4$ cup chili sauce
1 teaspoon grated onion
1 teaspoon Worcestershire
    sauce

MAKES $1^1/_4$ CUPS

Combine all ingredients together. Allow flavors to blend by chilling in covered jar at least 3 hours before serving.

Serving: 2 Tablespoons	Calories: 30	Protein: 1 gm
Calories from Fat: 3	Total Fat: 0.5 gm	Dietary Fiber: 0 gm
Saturated Fat: 0 gm	Carbs: 5 gm	Sodium: 190 mg
Component of Fat: 11%	Cholesterol: 1 mg	Calcium: 20 mg

Soups,
Stews
and
Chowders

CONTENTS

Northend Lobster Bouillabaisse

1 tablespoon olive oil
1 cup chopped onion
2 celery stalks, chopped
3 tomatoes, peeled,
    seeded and chopped
3 tablespoons fresh
    chopped parsley
1 bay leaf
1 teaspoon thyme
2 cups dry white wine
1 cup clam juice
2 tablespoons blanched
    almond slivers
2 cloves garlic
3 cups cooked lobster
    meat, cut into bite-
    sized pieces

SERVES 4

Heat olive oil in a large saucepan. Sauté onion and celery. Add tomatoes and simmer 5 minutes. Stir in parsley, bay leaf, thyme, white wine and clam juice. Bring to a boil, and simmer 20 minutes.

Grind almonds and garlic in blender or with a mortar and pestle. Add to simmering sauce, stir well. Cook another 15 minutes.

Pat lobster meat dry on paper towels. Add to bouillabaisse. Heat 10 minutes and serve.

Serving: 1/4 Recipe	Calories: 274	Protein: 24 gm
Calories from Fat: 57	Total Fat: 6 gm	Dietary Fiber: 2 gm
Saturated Fat: 1 gm	Carbs: 10 gm	Sodium: 663 mg
Component of Fat: 21%	Cholesterol: 78 mg	Calcium: 126 mg

Creamy Cold Cucumber Soup

2 cups peeled, seeded and
    diced cucumbers
2 teaspoons olive oil
1 tablespoon dill
1 clove garlic, minced
pinch of salt
1 teaspoon white pepper
$^3/_4$ cup non-fat plain
    yogurt
$1^1/_3$ cups non-fat sour
    cream

Garnish:
fresh lemons

SERVES 4

Combine cucumber, olive oil, dill, garlic, salt and pepper. Let stand 1 hour. Purée in blender. Fold in yogurt and sour cream. Chill at least 4 hours before serving.

Garnish each bowl with lemon slice or wedge.

Serving: 1/4 Recipe	Calories: 136	Protein: 6 gm
Calories from Fat: 22	Total Fat: 2.5 gm	Dietary Fiber: 1 gm
Saturated Fat: 0.5 gm	Carbs: 20 gm	Sodium: 157 mg
Component of Fat: 17%	Cholesterol: 1 mg	Calcium: 151 mg

Falmouth, Massachusetts, like most of Cape Cod, is a picturesque summer community. Founded by Quakers in 1661 on the principle of religious tolerance, its early economy was supported by whaling, shipbuilding and agriculture. Falmouth later become known for its fine glassworks. Local artisans continue the production of glass and crafts.

Vegetable Soup with Dumplings

3 cups assorted summer
    vegetables, chopped
    into bite-sized pieces
1 tablespoon safflower oil
1 cup low-sodium tomato
    juice
4 cups low-sodium
    vegetable broth

Dumplings:
1 cup cake flour
2 teaspoons double-acting
    baking powder
pinch of salt
1 egg
skim milk
1 tablespoon chopped
    fresh herbs

SERVES 8

Wash vegetables. Heat oil in large pot, add vegetables and tomato juice. Cover pot and cook on low heat. Heat broth in a separate pot, with tight-fitting lid.

Dumplings: Sift together flour, baking powder and salt. Break egg into a measuring cup, then add milk to make $1/2$ cup of liquid. Beat egg and milk together. Slowly stir milk mixture into flour. Batter will be stiff, and may require a little more milk to hold together. Stir in herbs.

When bouillon is boiling, dip a tablespoon in the broth. Form a dumpling in the spoon, drop it into the broth and cover pot. Re-dip spoon, and repeat process. Dumplings steam in about 10 minutes. They are done when a toothpick inserted in them comes out clean. Add broth and dumplings to vegetable stock.

Serving: 1/8 Recipe	Calories: 176	Protein: 5 gm
Calories from Fat: 40	Total Fat: 4.5 gm	Dietary Fiber: 3 gm
Saturated Fat: 1 gm	Carbs: 30 gm	Sodium: 676 mg
Component of Fat: 22%	Cholesterol: 27 mg	Calcium: 137 mg

Back Bay Clam Chowder

1 onion, chopped
2 teaspoons butter
2 tablespoons flour
2 cups clam juice
1 cup water
1 medium potato, diced
1 teaspoon thyme
2 cups skim milk blended
    with 1 cup non-fat
    powdered milk
2 cups shucked, steamed
    clam meats
salt and pepper to taste
parsley to taste

SERVES 6

Sauté onion in butter until clear. Blend in flour, then slowly mix in clam juice and water. Add diced potatoes and thyme. Simmer until potatoes are tender. Add milk and clams. Gently simmer 10 minutes, then serve.

Serving: 1/6 Recipe	Calories: 139	Protein: 12 gm
Calories from Fat: 17	Total Fat: 2 gm	Dietary Fiber: 1 gm
Saturated Fat: 1 gm	Carbs: 19 gm	Sodium: 202 mg
Component of Fat: 12%	Cholesterol: 16 mg	Calcium: 267 mg

COASTAL NEW ENGLAND   SUMMERTIME COOKING

Newport Harbor Lobster Stew

1 lb. lobster meat
1 clove garlic, minced
2 teaspoons butter
3 tablespoons cognac
2 tablespoons pignoli
    nuts, chopped
2 cups fish broth
1 cup dry white wine
1 tablespoon lemon juice
1 teaspoon basil
1 teaspoon pepper

SERVES 5

Cut lobster meat into bite-sized pieces and sauté with garlic in butter. Stir in cognac and chopped pignoli nuts. Add remaining ingredients and simmer 10 minutes.

Serving: 1/5 Recipe
Calories from Fat: 45
Saturated Fat: 2 gm
Component of Fat: 24%

Calories: 191
Total Fat: 5 gm
Carbs: 3 gm
Cholesterol: 90 mg

Protein: 20 gm
Dietary Fiber: 0 gm
Sodium: 597 mg
Calcium: 88 mg

Caldeirada
(Portuguese Seafood Soup)

1 tablespoon olive oil
2 cups chopped onion
1/2 cup chopped pepper
2 cloves garlic, minced
3 medium-sized potatoes,
    peeled, halved, and cut
    in thick slices
3 cups fish broth
3 cups dry white wine
2 cups cooked, chopped
    and drained spinach
2 cups crushed tomatoes
1 tablespoon
    Worcestershire sauce
1 teaspoon pepper
1 lb. mackerel or bluefish,
    cut in small chunks

SERVES 6

In a large pot, sauté onion, pepper and garlic in olive oil. When onions are clear, stir in potatoes, cover pot, and cook 5 minutes over medium heat. Add fish broth, wine, spinach, tomatoes, Worcestershire sauce and pepper. Simmer until potatoes are tender.

Add chunks of fish and cook 15 minutes, or until fish is opaque. Do not overcook. Serve at once.

Serving: 1/6 Recipe
Calories from Fat: 59
Saturated Fat: 1 gm
Component of Fat: 19%

Calories: 312
Total Fat: 7 gm
Carbs: 28 gm
Cholesterol: 45 mg

Protein: 24 gm
Dietary Fiber: 6 gm
Sodium: 721 mg
Calcium: 193 mg

In the 18th and 19th centuries, many Azorean Portuguese fisherman settled on the coast of Massachusetts. Their influence on New England cooking has contributed vibrancy and flavor. In addition to seafood, the crusty Portuguese breads are popular on Cape Cod and Nantucket. New Bedford celebrates Portuguese cuisine with the Saint's Day feasts.

Oyster Stew

Northeastern oysters are large and flavorful. If purchasing opened oysters, they should be plump and creamy, and their liquor clear.

SERVES 6

1 tablespoon butter
1 tablespoon sherry
1 tablespoon grated onion
$1/4$ cup diced celery
$1/2$ teaspoon minced garlic
1 tablespoon flour
3 cups skim milk
blended with 1 cup
non-fat powdered
milk
$1/2$ cup skimmed
evaporated milk
3 cups oysters and their
liquor (see below)
salt and pepper to taste
1 tablespoon parsley

Boil water in the bottom pan of a double boiler. In the top pan, heat butter and sherry. Add onion, celery and garlic, and cook until clear. Blend in flour. Slowly whisk in milks, stirring until smooth.

Add oysters and their liquor, salt and pepper. Cook stew, without boiling, until milk is hot and oysters float. Sprinkle parsley over stew. Serve at once, so oysters do not overcook.

Serving: 1/6 Recipe	Calories: 212	Protein: 19 gm
Calories from Fat: 48	Total Fat: 5.5 gm	Dietary Fiber: 0 gm
Saturated Fat: 2 gm	Carbs: 21 gm	Sodium: 350 mg
Component of Fat: 23%	Cholesterol: 78 mg	Calcium: 416 mg

Preparing oysters: Scrub well, discard any that do not close tightly or have broken shells. To easily open oysters, place in 400° oven for 6 minutes, plunge into ice water, then drain. Oysters can now be easily opened. Use a knife to release flesh from the shell, reserving juice (oyster liquor). Strain liquor through fine muslin to remove grit.

Shrimp Bisque

³/₄ lb. small salad shrimp
3 cups skim milk blended
    with 1 cup non-fat
    powdered milk
1 cup skimmed
    evaporated milk
¼ cup grated onion
¼ cup finely chopped
    celery
¼ cup finely chopped
    carrots
1 teaspoon butter
2 tablespoons sherry
3 tablespoons flour
2 tablespoons tomato
    paste
salt and pepper to taste

SERVES 6

Clean and wash shrimp, check to be sure shells are removed. Simmer shrimp in milk for 10 minutes.

In a saucepan, cook onion, celery and carrot in butter until soft, but do not brown. Add sherry, then blend in flour, tomato paste, salt and pepper. Over low heat, whisk in milk and shrimp mixture until well blended.

Tranfer to blender and process until completely smooth. Return to pot and heat until thickened, but do not boil.

Serving: 1/6 Recipe
Calories from Fat: 17
Saturated Fat: 1 gm
Component of Fat: 8%

Calories: 210
Total Fat: 2 gm
Carbs: 22 gm
Cholesterol: 118 mg

Protein: 24 gm
Dietary Fiber: 1 gm
Sodium: 419 mg
Calcium: 443 mg

COASTAL NEW ENGLAND   SUMMERTIME COOKING

Curried Carrot Soup

1 lb. carrots
2 teaspoons butter
1/2 cup chopped yellow
    onion
3 cups vegetable bouillon
    broth
1/2 cup dry white rice
2 teaspoons curry powder
1/3 cup skimmed
    evaporated milk
salt and pepper to taste

SERVES 4

Peel carrots and slice into 1-inch pieces. Sauté onion in butter until clear, but do not brown. Add carrots to bouillon and bring to a boil. Reduce heat, add rice and simmer until carrots are very tender, about 30 minutes. Purée in blender with sautéed onion. Return to pot, stir in curry, evaporated milk, salt and pepper.

Serving: 1/4 Recipe
Calories from Fat: 21
Saturated Fat: 1 gm
Component of Fat: 15%

Calories: 139
Total Fat: 2.5 gm
Carbs: 27 gm
Cholesterol: 6 mg

Protein: 4 gm
Dietary Fiber: 4 gm
Sodium: 176 mg
Calcium: 103 mg

Lentil Soup

1 lb. dry lentils
8 cups weak vegetable
   bouillon broth
1 cup chopped onion
1 cup peeled and diced
   carrots
1 cup diced celery
2 cloves garlic, minced
1 teaspoon fresh ground
   pepper
$^1/_2$ teaspoon curry
1 tablespoon chopped
   fresh cilantro
2 cups peeled and chopped
   tomatoes
2 bay leaves
2 tablespoons vinegar

SERVES 6

Rinse lentils in cold water. Combine all ingredients in large covered pot. Stirring occasionally, simmer about 3 hours, adding water if needed. Discard bay leaves. Adjust seasonings to taste. Serve hot.

Serving: 1/6 Recipe
Calories from Fat: 10
Saturated Fat: 0 gm
Component of Fat: 9%

Calories: 337
Total Fat: 1 gm
Carbs: 62 gm
Cholesterol: 0 mg

Protein: 24 gm
Dietary Fiber: 2 gm
Sodium: 260 mg
Calcium: 86 mg

Hearty Vegetable Minestrone

1 cup dried kidney beans
5 cups vegetable broth
3 cups water
2 cups tomato purée
1 leek, white stalk only
1 tablespoon olive oil
1 cup diced onion
1 clove garlic, minced
1 cup shredded cabbage
1 cup chopped carrots
1 cup diced zucchini
1 cup fresh shelled peas
1 cup chopped Italian
    plum tomatoes
1 tablespoon oregano
1/3 cup chopped parsley
1 cup elbow macaroni
1/2 cup grated Parmesan
    cheese

SERVES 8

Soak kidney beans in cold water, then boil in broth, water and tomato purée until tender.

Wash leek thoroughly, and dice. Sauté leek, onion and garlic in olive oil. Add cabbage, carrots and zucchini. Cook over medium-high heat 10 minutes. Add cooked vegetables, peas, chopped tomatoes and spices to broth.

Bring to a full boil and add elbow macaroni. Simmer 30 minutes. Serve bowls with a tablespoon of grated Parmesan cheese.

Serving: 1/8 Recipe	Calories: 274	Protein: 14 gm
Calories from Fat: 57	Total Fat: 6 gm	Dietary Fiber: 11 gm
Saturated Fat: 3 gm	Carbs: 43 gm	Sodium: 366 mg
Component of Fat: 20%	Cholesterol: 10 mg	Calcium: 220 mg

Rhode Island's public beaches include Hazard's Beach and Gooseberry Beach in Newport, and Suchuest and Third Beach in Middletown. The Visitor's Bureau offers self-guided walking tours of colonial Newport, highlighting its naval and architectural history. Summer festivities in Newport include the Newport Music, Folk and Jazz Festivals.

Cream of Asparagus

5 medium-sized potatoes
2 lbs. asparagus
2 leeks, white stalks only
2 cups water
2 cups dry white wine
salt and pepper to taste
skim milk, optional

SERVES 4

Peel and quarter potatoes. Remove dry base ends of asparagus, then cut stalks into 1-inch pieces. Wash leeks stalks well, and cut into 1-inch pieces. Place potatoes, asparagus, leeks, water and wine in covered pot. Simmer until very soft. Process vegetables and cooking water through food mill (or food processor, but texture will be bland.) Stir in salt and pepper. If desired, thin with a little milk.

Serving: 1/4 Recipe	Calories: 300	Protein: 11 gm
Calories from Fat: 16	Total Fat: 2 gm	Dietary Fiber: 7 gm
Saturated Fat: 0 gm	Carbs: 41 gm	Sodium: 88 mg
Component of Fat: 5%	Cholesterol: 0 mg	Calcium: 98 mg

Quick Gazpacho

1 cup peeled, seeded and
    finely diced cucumber
2 cups skinned, seeded
    and finely chopped
    tomatoes
1 cup vegetable broth
1 cup crushed tomatoes
2 tablespoons diced
    pimento
2 teaspoons olive oil
$^1/_2$ red pepper, grated
1 tablespoon fresh dill
pinch of cayenne
1 tablespoon finely
    chopped chives
salt and pepper to taste

SERVES 4

Combine half of the cucumber, tomatoes, vegetable broth, crushed tomatoes and pimento in blender. Process 2 minutes. Add olive oil and blend another minute.

Pour into a bowl and stir in remaining cucumber, tomatoes, broth, pimento and other ingredients. Chill well before serving.

Serving: 1/4 Recipe
Calories from Fat: 25
Saturated Fat: 0.5 gm
Component of Fat: 25%

Calories: 90
Total Fat: 3 gm
Carbs: 15 gm
Cholesterol: 0 mg

Protein: 3 gm
Dietary Fiber: 3 gm
Sodium: 250 mg
Calcium: 43 mg

Rocky Neck Chilled Seafood Stew

Rocky Neck State Park in Connecticut has a mile long crescent beach, boardwalk and fishing. Bring along this stew for a cool picnic supper.

2 cups cooked and
   chopped seafood,
     such as shrimp, crab,
     clams and salmon
$\frac{1}{2}$ cup chopped celery
$\frac{1}{4}$ cup grated sweet red or
   purple onion
$\frac{1}{2}$ cup finely chopped
   pepper
$\frac{1}{2}$ cup chopped, peeled
   and seeded cucumber
2 cups plum tomatoes,
   chopped
3 tablespoons fresh
   chopped parsley
2 cups low-sodium tomato
   or vegetable juice
1 cup white wine
2 tablespoons lemon juice
1 teaspoon pepper
1 teaspoon Worcestershire
   sauce

SERVES 6

Chill seafood in large covered bowl. Combine remaining ingredients in large pot. Simmer for 20 minutes. Cool at room temperature, then fold into fish. Chill thoroughly, and serve.

Serving: 1/6 Recipe
Calories from Fat: 10
Saturated Fat: 0 gm
Component of Fat: 8%

Calories: 120
Total Fat: 1 gm
Carbs: 12 gm
Cholesterol: 64 mg

Protein: 11 gm
Dietary Fiber: 3 gm
Sodium: 478 mg
Calcium: 52 mg

Main Meal Dishes

CONTENTS

Any fish cooked by any means, generally requires only 10 minutes of cooking time for each inch of thickness at its thickest part.

COASTAL NEW ENGLAND　　SUMMERTIME COOKING

Char-Blackened Bluefish

Any firm-fleshed fish is excellent on the grill. Bluefish is very dense,
and other types of fish may require a little less cooking time.

4 bluefish fillets or
    tuna steaks, sized
    to suit appetites
1 cup non-fat mayonnaise
1 tablespoon paprika
1 tablespoon lemon juice
1 teaspoon olive oil
pinch of celery salt
1 teaspoon pepper

SERVES 4

Remove grill from barbeque. Build fire and let it burn down to hot coals. Lower rack to about 2 inches above coals. Spray grill with non-stick oil. Pat fish fillets dry with towel.

Blend together mayonnaise, paprika, lemon juice, olive oil, salt and pepper.

Place a thin coat of basting sauce on one side of fillets. Place basted side down on the grill. Coat upper side of fish with thick layer of sauce. Grill 4 minutes, then flip fish. Baste top side with thick layer of sauce. When bottom side of fish is blackened, flip and on first side again, until blackened.

: 1/4 Recipe	Calories: 162	Protein: 17 gm
s from Fat: 45	Total Fat: 5 gm	Dietary Fiber: 0 gm
ed Fat: 1 gm	Carbs: 10 gm	Sodium: 491 mg
nent of Fat: 29%	Cholesterol: 50 mg	Calcium: 11 mg

The Lobster Bake by Sunset

Choose a gravel or sandy area, and start your preparations mid-day. You'll be rewarded with these gifts from the sea at sunset.

6 cups sea water
seaweed rinsed of sand,
    or leaves of 1 head
    iceberg lettuce
6 dozen steamer clams
6 lobsters, 1-1½ lbs. each
6 ears of corn, husked
6 potatoes wrapped in
    double layers of foil

Serve seafood with:
bowls of lemon juice and
    clam juice with salt
    and pepper to taste

Bring along:
corn and potato fixings
lobster crackers and picks

SERVES 6

This meal can also be prepared on a stove top.

Preparation: Scrub clams, discarding any with broken shells or that do not close tightly when handled. Tie clams by the dozen, in squares of cheesecloth tied with string. Allow room in bags for clams to open.

Dig a 3 foot deep hole in the sand or gravel. Build a fire of driftwood. Let it die down and turn to hot coals about 2 hours before sunset. Set 24-quart steamer pot in hole over embers. Pour sea water into pot and place 2 inches of seaweed or lettuce leaves in water.

Place lobsters and corn in pot. Cover with 4-inches rinsed seaweed or lettuce. Put clam bags on seaweed and cover pot. Place wrapped baking potatoes around base of pot. Fill in hole with sand or gravel, covering potatoes and pot. Leave covered about 1½ hours. Carefully dig up lobster pot and potatoes.

Serving: 1/6 Recipe	Calories: 429	Protein: 53 gm
Calories from Fat: 34	Total Fat: 4 gm	Dietary Fiber: 5 gm
Saturated Fat: 1 gm	Carbs: 48 gm	Sodium: 690 mg
Component of Fat: 8%	Cholesterol: 208 mg	Calcium: 147 mg

COASTAL NEW ENGLAND   SUMMERTIME COOKING

How to Eat
Lobster and Clams

Lobster: Bend back claws and flippers, break off where attached to body. Use cracker and pick to remove meat in claws and knuckles. Suck meat from flippers.

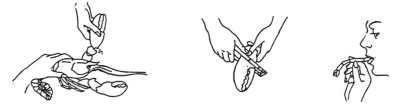

Bend back tail and break off from body. Tail flippers can also be broken back and the meat pushed out, or you can cut the membrane. In the body are the green tomalley (liver) and the red coral of the females (roe).

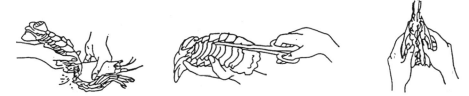

Clams: Wedge open shells and loosen meat. Dip in broth to rinse off sand.

Broiled Mussels

6 dozen mussels
3 egg whites
1 tablespoon olive oil
4 tablespoons fresh
     chopped parsley
1 teaspoon garlic powder
$^3/_4$ cup fine, plain bread
     crumbs

Serve with:
lemon wedges

SERVES 4

Scrub mussels, discarding any that do not close or have broken shells. Yank off beards. Steam in a covered pot until open, about 10 minutes. Drain. Open mussels and detach meat from shells, setting aside half of the shells. Pat mussel meat dry. Combine egg whites and oil in bowl, add mussels and stir to coat.

Preheat broiler. Combine parsley, garlic and bread crumbs in a bowl. Add mussels and toss. Let mussels set in crumbs 20 minutes, then place each in a half-shell. Set in baking pan and sprinkle remaining crumbs over mussels. Place on upper rack of broiler until light crust forms.

Serving: 1/4 Recipe	Calories: 351	Protein: 16 gm
Calories from Fat: 180	Total Fat: 20 gm	Dietary Fiber: 2 gm
Saturated Fat: 5 gm	Carbs: 28 gm	Sodium: 620 mg
Component of Fat: 50%	Cholesterol: 103 mg	Calcium: 120 mg

Blue mussels are dredged from shallow muddy bays of coastal New England, and harvested from tidal ponds and salty river beds. Mussels must be kept chilled to stay fresh. Check mussels by trying to slide the two halves of the shell across each other. If they move, discard, along with any that have broken shells, or that do not close when handled.

Brandied Shrimp Scampi

2 teaspoons butter
2 teaspoons olive oil
3 cloves pressed garlic
4 scallions, white stalks
    only, chopped fine
1½ lbs. shrimp, peeled
    and deveined
2 teaspoons lemon juice
3 tablespoons brandy
salt and pepper to taste

Optional:
oven-toasted sesame seeds

SERVES 4

Spray a large skillet with non-stick oil. Heat butter and olive oil in skillet, then add pressed garlic and chopped scallions.

Pat dry shrimp in a towel. Raise heat under pan, toss in shrimp and sear. Shake and toss shrimp in pan to brown on all sides.

Before removing from heat, sprinkle shrimp with lemon juice and brandy. The liquid should evaporate, but the flavors will remain. Toss with salt and pepper. If desired, sprinkle with toasted sesame seeds.

Serving: 1/4 Recipe
Calories from Fat: 50
Saturated Fat: 2 gm
Component of Fat: 24%

Calories: 201
Total Fat: 6 gm
Carbs: 8 gm
Cholesterol: 52 mg

Protein: 22 gm
Dietary Fiber: 0 gm
Sodium: 616 mg
Calcium: 74 mg

Gay Head Cliffs
Martha's Vineyard,
Massachusetts

Skewered Braised Scallops

1¹/₂ lbs. medium-sized
    scallops (or large sea
    scallops cut in half)

Baste #1:
4 tablespoons miso paste
2 tablespoons lemon juice
5 tablespoons red wine

Baste #2:
3 tablespoons tamari or
    soy sauce
4 tablespoons lemon juice
3 tablespoons flour
4 tablespoons white wine

SERVES 4

Preheat broiler. Rinse scallops and pat dry.

Blend your baste of choice. The consistency should be thick, but spreadable.

Place scallops on flat, double-edged skewers, with space between them. Coat with baste. Rest ends of skewers on rim of deep baking pan (so scallops do not touch pan, but drippings are caught.) Broil on upper rack. Turn scallops to brown on all sides, basting as needed. Scallops will cook in 10-12 minutes.

Serving: 1/4 Recipe	Calories: 163	Protein: 29 gm
Calories from Fat: 14	Total Fat: 2 gm	Dietary Fiber: 0 gm
Saturated Fat: 0 gm	Carbs: 6 gm	Sodium: 431 mg
Component of Fat: 9%	Cholesterol: 56 mg	Calcium: 44 mg

Crab Soufflé

1 teaspoon flour
1 cup skim milk blended
   with $^1/_2$ cup non-fat
   powdered milk
1 tablespoon butter
1 tablespoon canola oil
4 tablespoons flour
2 eggs, separated
2 egg whites
pinch of curry
pinch of dry mustard
$^1/_2$ teaspoon white pepper
$1^1/_2$ lbs. crab meat,
   fresh or canned

SERVES 6

Preheat oven to 375°. Surround a 2-quart soufflé dish with a collar made of a double-layer of aluminum foil, extending 2 inches above rim of dish.   Secure collar with a straight pin pointed downwards. Spray with non-stick oil, and dust with 1 teaspoon flour.

Put milk in small pot to boil. In a saucepan, melt butter with oil, then blend in 4 tablespoons flour. Quickly pour boiling milk into flour roux and whisk until thick and smooth. Remove from heat and cool slightly.

Beat in egg yolks, curry, mustard and pepper. Break apart crab meat and fold in. With an electric beater, beat the 4 egg whites until stiff. Fold into crab mixture. Pour into soufflé dish. Bake 35-40 minutes or until golden. (Do not open oven until done!) Remove collar and serve.

Serving: 1/6 Recipe
Calories from Fat: 69
Saturated Fat: 2 gm
Component of Fat: 32%

Calories: 222
Total Fat: 8 gm
Carbs: 10 gm
Cholesterol: 176 mg

Protein: 27 gm
Dietary Fiber: 0 gm
Sodium: 384 mg
Calcium: 231 mg

Lobster Pie

4 cups cooked lobster
    meat, cut into bite-
    sized pieces
1 tablespoon melted
    unsalted butter
3 tablespoons vermouth
1 tablepoon fresh chopped
    parsley
$\frac{1}{2}$ teaspoon white salt
$\frac{1}{2}$ teaspoon white pepper
2 teaspoons canola oil
$1\frac{1}{2}$ cups bread crumbs

SERVES 4

Preheat oven to 350°. Spray 4 individual casserole dishes with non-stick oil.

Toss lobster meat with melted butter, vermouth, parsley, salt and white pepper. Put lobster into prepared casserole dishes.

Mix bread crumbs with canola oil. Sprinkle over lobster. Bake until tops are lightly browned.

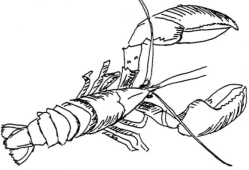

Serving: 1/4 Recipe
Calories from Fat: 62
Saturated Fat: 2 gm
Component of Fat: 26%

Calories: 246
Total Fat: 7 gm
Carbs: 10 gm
Cholesterol: 112 mg

Protein: 31 gm
Dietary Fiber: 0 gm
Sodium: 670 mg
Calcium: 115 mg

During the War of 1812, two British men-o-war came in view off the sound of New London. In nearby Fort Griswold, preparations ran amuck when it was discovered there was a shortage of flannel cloth to load and pack the cannons. Much of the town had been evacuated, but colonist soldiers ran through the streets knocking on doors. (cont.)

COASTAL NEW ENGLAND SUMMERTIME COOKING

Sole Amandine

2 tablespoons almond
    slivers
1¹/₂ lbs. fillets of sole
2 teaspoons butter
1 teaspoon canola oil
2 tablespoons white wine
1 tablespoon lemon juice
salt and pepper to taste

SERVES 4

Toast almond slices on cookie sheet in oven until lightly browned.

Spray large pan with non-stick oil. On medium heat, warm butter and oil. Fry sole on both sides. After turning to second side, sprinkle with wine, lemon juice, salt and pepper. Spread toasted almond slices on fillets of sole.

Serving: 1/4 Recipe	Calories: 252	Protein: 42 gm
Calories from Fat: 68	Total Fat: 8 gm	Dietary Fiber: 0 gm
Saturated Fat: 2 gm	Carbs: 1 gm	Sodium: 225 mg
Component of Fat: 28%	Cholesterol: 120 mg	Calcium: 42 mg

(cont.) Mrs. Anna Warner Bailey answered her door and listened to the soldier's plea. When they finished, she dropped her red flannel petticoat to the ground at their feet. The soldiers returned with the petticoat, which was hoisted on a pikestaff as a tribute to the unique contribution. Then-after she was called "Mother Bailey," and regarded a heroine of the war.

COASTAL NEW ENGLAND   SUMMERTIME COOKING

Flounder Florentine

1¹/₂ lbs. flounder fillets
1 lb. fresh spinach
1 tablespoon canola oil
2 tablespoons white wine
3 tablespoons grated
    onion
2 tablespoons flour
1 cup skim milk blended
    with ¹/₂ cup non-fat
    powdered milk
pinch of ground cloves
pinch of nutmeg
1 teaspoon Worcestershire
    sauce
salt and pepper to taste
1 tablespoon parsley

SERVES 4

Poach the flounder fillets by steaming them over boiling water until springy to the touch.

Remove stems from spinach. Chop or tear leaves. Steam just until wilted. Place spinach in a sieve, press out moisture and drain.

In a saucepan, heat oil and wine, then sauté grated onion. Blend in flour. Whisk in milk and stirring constantly, cook until thick and smooth. Add remaining spices, stir well.

Preheat oven to 350°. Spray baking pan with non-stick oil. Spread spinach in pan, arrange flounder on top. Pour sauce over flounder. Bake just long enough to heat through.

Serving: 1/4 Recipe	Calories: 329	Protein: 50 gm
Calories from Fat: 60	Total Fat: 7 gm	Dietary Fiber: 3 gm
Saturated Fat: 1 gm	Carbs: 15 gm	Sodium: 386 mg
Component of Fat: 18%	Cholesterol: 118 mg	Calcium: 329 mg

COASTAL NEW ENGLAND   SUMMERTIME COOKING

Halibut with Parsley Sauce

1¹/₂ lbs. fresh halibut
   steaks
1 teaspoon melted butter
2 teaspoons olive oil
2 cloves garlic, halved
1 tablespoon flour
³/₄ cup low-fat buttermilk
¹/₂ teaspoon white pepper
¹/₄ teaspoon salt
3 tablespoons fresh
   chopped parsley
1 tablespoon lemon juice

SERVES 4

Preheat broiler or prepare grill. Use non-stick oil to spray broiler pan, or grill before placing on fire. Put halibut on pan or grill, brush lightly with melted butter. Cook on both sides, brushing second side with butter when turned.

In a saucepan, heat olive oil with garlic. When garlic has browned, stir, and remove from oil. Blend flour into hot oil. Whisk in buttermilk, stirring until sauce is thick and smooth. Add white pepper, salt and parsley. Remove from heat and stir in lemon juice. To serve, spoon Parsley Sauce over halibut.

Serving: 1/4 Recipe	Calories: 227	Protein: 36 gm
Calories from Fat: 64	Total Fat: 7 gm	Dietary Fiber: 0 gm
Saturated Fat: 1 gm	Carbs: 3 gm	Sodium: 237 mg
Component of Fat: 29%	Cholesterol: 57 mg	Calcium: 89 mg

Summer Vegie Accents: When poaching fish add slices of select fall herbs and vegetables that will not overpower the fish. Try fresh carrots, celery, summer squash and dill (avoid strong scents like broccoli). Fish and vegetables will enhance each other's flavors. Cut vegetables into pieces that will cook in the same amount of time as your fish.

Codfish Cakes

1 lb. salt codfish
3 cups water
1 large carrot, quartered
1 onion, quartered
1 celery stalk, quartered
1 garlic clove, halved
1 bay leaf
3 medium-sized potatoes,
   quartered
1 teaspoon grated lemon
   rind
$1/4$ cup grated onion
1 teaspoon pepper
1 egg
1 tablespoon skim milk
2 tablespoons flour
2 tablespoons safflower
   oil
Serve with: lemon wedges

SERVES 4

Soak salted codfish in cold water for 6 hours, pounding and rinsing fish, and changing water every hour to remove the salt.

Boil 3 cups water with carrot, onion, celery, garlic, bay leaf and potatoes. Simmer 15 minutes. Wrap codfish in a cheesecloth and simmer 5 minutes in broth. Remove pot from heat, leaving fish in hot broth 10 minutes more, then remove and pat dry. Return pot to heat and continue cooking potatoes until tender.

Put codfish in bowl and use two forks to flake into shreds. Put potatoes in a separate bowl and mash. Combine potatoes, lemon rind, grated onion, pepper, egg, milk and flour with codfish. Form into 3-inch cakes. Preheat frying pan, spray with non-stick oil and coat with oil. Fry codfish cakes until browned.

Serving: 1/4 Recipe	Calories: 325	Protein: 32 gm
Calories from Fat: 84	Total Fat: 9 gm	Dietary Fiber: 5 gm
Saturated Fat: 1 gm	Carbs: 30 gm	Sodium: 415 mg
Component of Fat: 25%	Cholesterol: 116 mg	Calcium: 77 mg

Maple-Mustard Salmon

1½ lbs. fresh salmon
    fillets
2 tablespoons Dijon
    mustard
¼ cup maple syrup
1 teaspoon lemon juice
1 teaspoon white pepper
pinch of salt
1 teaspoon melted butter

SERVES 4

Preheat broiler. Check salmon fillets for bones and remove with pliers. Blend mustard, maple syrup, lemon juice, pepper and salt.

Spray broiler pan with non-stick oil. Place fillets on pan and brush with butter. Coat with maple-mustard sauce. Place under broiler, leaving oven door tipped open. Salmon is done when inner flesh is light pink. Serve with juices from pan spooned over fish.

Sauce can also be used to baste salmon on outside grill.

Serving: 1/4 Recipe
Calories from Fat: 62
Saturated Fat: 2 gm
Component of Fat: 24%

Calories: 257
Total Fat: 7 gm
Carbs: 13 gm
Cholesterol: 91 mg

Protein: 34 gm
Dietary Fiber: 0 gm
Sodium: 152 mg
Calcium: 32 mg

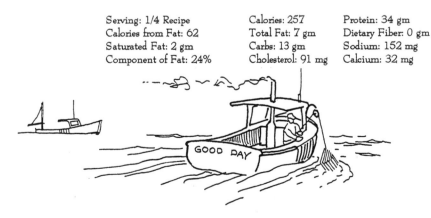

GOOD DAY

Poached Salmon
with Dill Sauce

1½ lbs. fresh salmon
    fillets
1½ cups white wine
1 teaspoon butter
2 teaspoons flour
1 teaspoon white pepper
1 tablespoon fresh dill
1 tablepoon lemon juice
pinch of cayenne
pinch of salt

SERVES 4

Cut salmon fillets into 4 portions. In a large saucepan, bring white wine to a simmer. Place fillets in saucepan, cover. Poach 12 minutes, or until the inner flesh has turned light pink. Remove salmon with slotted spatula, cover and place in 250° oven.

Combine hot poaching wine in blender with remaining ingredients. Process for 1 minute. Return to saucepan, and whisk until thickened.

Serve poached salmon fillets with dill sauce spooned on top.

Serving: 1/4 Recipe
Calories from Fat: 62
Saturated Fat: 2 gm
Component of Fat: 23%

Calories: 275
Total Fat: 7 gm
Carbs: 2 gm
Cholesterol: 91 mg

Protein: 34 gm
Dietary Fiber: 0 gm
Sodium: 155 mg
Calcium: 21 mg

Oven-Fried Swordfish

1 tablespoon olive oil
1¹/₂ lbs. fresh swordfish
    steaks
2 egg whites
¹/₂ cup cornmeal
1 teaspoon pepper
pinch of salt
1 teaspoon garlic powder

SERVES 4

Preheat oven to 400°. Spray a large baking pan with non-stick oil and coat with olive oil.

Cut swordfish steaks into 4 servings. Pat dry on paper towels. Beat egg whites. Pour into shallow pan. Place swordfish into egg mixture to coat all sides. Mix cornmeal and spices together. Dip swordfish in cornmeal to lightly coat both sides, then place in baking pan.

Bake in preheated oven, turning once after bottom side has browned. Swordfish is ready as soon as inside of steaks are opaque.

Serving: 1/4 Recipe	Calories: 289	Protein: 37 gm
Calories from Fat: 72	Total Fat: 8 gm	Dietary Fiber: 1 gm
Saturated Fat: 2 gm	Carbs: 14 gm	Sodium: 207 mg
Component of Fat: 26%	Cholesterol: 66 mg	Calcium: 13 mg

Most New England towns contain a "Green" or "Common." The grassy, central square of small towns, the green often has a bandstand, gazebo or monument. Originally a livestock assembly area from which animals would be brought to open pastureland by the town herdsmen, a town's green later became a focal point for outdoor community activities.

Seafood Newburg

SERVES 6

1 lb. flounder or sole
$1/_2$ lb. shrimp, peeled and
    deveined
$1/_2$ lb. small bay scallops
1 teaspoon butter
2 tablespoons finely
    chopped shallots
$1/_2$ cup Madeira
2 cups skim milk blended
    with 1 cup non-fat
    powdered milk
3 egg yolks
1 tablespoon tomato paste
salt and white pepper
6 slices toast, halved

Poach flounder, shrimp and scallops in boiling water for 8-10 minutes. Drain well. Peel skin off flounder or sole, and cut fish into bite-sized pieces.

Heat butter in saucepan. Sauté shallots for 5 minutes. Stir in Madeira and heat.

Beat milk with egg yolks. Whisk into shallot mixture, stirring constantly while sauce thickens. Add tomato paste, salt and white pepper to taste. Gently fold in fish and heat. Serve Newburg over sliced toast halves.

Serving: 1/6 Recipe	Calories: 364	Protein: 45 gm
Calories from Fat: 61	Total Fat: 7 gm	Dietary Fiber: 1 gm
Saturated Fat: 2 gm	Carbs: 24 gm	Sodium: 501 mg
Component of Fat: 17%	Cholesterol: 241 mg	Calcium: 364 mg

Off the Connecticut coast in Long Island Sound, bluefish, striped bass and flounder are plentiful. Many towns along the shore rent fishing boats and equipment. The Thames, Housatonic and Connecticut Rivers, along with dozens of small streams and lakes also offer freshwater fishing. Most of these freshwater bodies are annually stocked with brook trout.

Pasta, Beans, and Grains

CONTENTS

Any Pasta, Beans and Grains recipe can be used for a main dish or side dish by varying the amount per person.

Chilled Providence Primavera

Heavenly on a warm evening, or, if preferred, serve Primavera hot.

SERVES 4

$^1/_2$ cup finely chopped purple onion
1 cup chopped red pepper
1 cup snow peas, cut diagonally in 1-inch pieces
$^1/_4$ cup chopped scallions
8 black olives, chopped
6 ripe plum tomatoes, peeled and chopped
$^1/_2$ cup red wine vinegar
2 cups tomato purée
1 tablespoon fresh basil
1 tablespoon oregano
1 teaspoon black pepper
2 cloves garlic, minced
2 teaspoons grated lime zest
1 lb. fettucine noodles
2 teaspoons safflower oil
6 tablespoons grated Parmesan cheese

In a large saucepan, combine vegetables, vinegar, tomato purée, spices and lime zest. Simmer at least at hour, until a small amount put on a plate does not show a rim of liquid separating from sauce. Chill.

Boil fettucine noodles until tender. Drain. Toss with safflower oil. Cover and chill.

When pasta and sauce have thoroughly chilled, divide fettucine among plates and ladle primavera sauce on top. Sprinkle with grated Parmesan cheese.

Serving: 1/4 Recipe	Calories: 650	Protein: 22 gm
Calories from Fat: 82	Total Fat: 9 gm	Dietary Fiber: 10 gm
Saturated Fat: 2 gm	Carbs: 120 gm	Sodium: 422 mg
Component of Fat: 12%	Cholesterol: 6 mg	Calcium: 239 mg

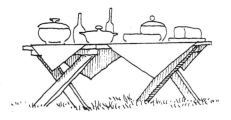

Pesto and Angel Hair Pasta

1½ packed cups fresh
  basil leaves
1 tablespoon olive oil
1 tablespoon lemon juice
1½ tablespoons pine nuts
1 clove garlic, minced
1 teaspoon white pepper
3 tablespoons fresh grated
  Parmesan cheese
2 tablespoons grated
  Romano cheese
2 lbs. fresh refrigerated
  angel hair pasta
2 tablespoons pasta water

SERVES 6

With blender running on high speed, carefully drop in basil leaves, olive oil, lemon juice, pine nuts, garlic and pepper. Stop blender as needed to scrape mixture down from sides. Process until well blended. Pour into a bowl and stir in grated cheese.

Boil angel hair pasta until tender. Remove 2 tablespoons of the boiled water and mix it into the pesto. Drain pasta. Toss pasta with desired amount of pesto, or divide pasta among serving plates and spoon pesto on top.

Serving: 1/6 Recipe
Calories from Fat: 96
Saturated Fat: 3 gm
Component of Fat: 18%

Calories: 514
Total Fat: 11 gm
Carbs: 83 gm
Cholesterol: 175 mg

Protein: 22 gm
Dietary Fiber: 4 gm
Sodium: 132 mg
Calcium: 117 mg

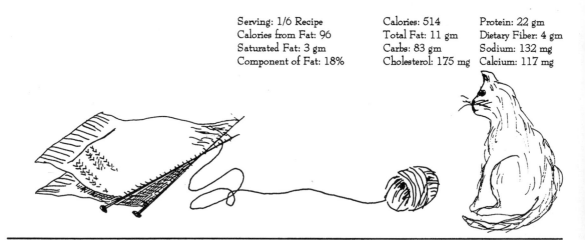

Lobster Ravioli

Making home-made ravioli requires a pasta machine and pastry crimper. If you enjoy fresh pasta, they are worth-while investments.

1 cup all-purpose flour
1 egg
1 tablespoon water
pinch of salt
1 teaspoon safflower oil
2 cups peeleed tomatoes
    and their juice
$1/2$ cup red wine
3 tablespoons tomato
    paste
2 tablespoons chopped
    fresh tarragon leaves
1 clove garlic, minced
$1/4$ cup skim milk
$1/4$ cup non-fat dry
    powdered milk
2 cups lobster meat, cut
    into small pieces
2 tablespoons grated
    Parmesan cheese
1 teaspoon black pepper

SERVES 4

Combine flour, egg, water, salt and oil with your fingers or in food processor, until well blended. Following manufacturer's directions, process through pasta machine into sheets.

Finely dice tomatoes. In a saucepan, combine tomatoes and their juices, wine, tomato paste, tarragon and garlic. Boil down until thickened. Whisk together skim and powdered milks, then stir into tomato sauce and reduce heat.

Mix $1/2$ cup sauce with lobster, Parmesan and pepper. On a sheet of pasta dough, space 3 tablespoons lobster filling 5-inches apart from each other. Cover with top sheet. Use pastry crimper to cut into 4-inch squares. Boil ravioli 2-3 minutes in salted water.

Ladle tomato sauce onto each serving plate. Place ravioli on tomato sauce. Serve hot.

Serving: 1/4 Recipe	Calories: 268	Protein: 19 gm
Calories from Fat: 29	Total Fat: 3 gm	Dietary Fiber: 2 gm
Saturated Fat: 1 gm	Carbs: 36 gm	Sodium: 506 mg
Component of Fat: 11%	Cholesterol: 57 mg	Calcium: 185 mg

Lasagne with Roasted Bell Peppers

1 lb. red bell peppers
1 lb. green bell peppers
2 teaspoons olive oil
1 onion, chopped
2 cloves minced garlic
16 oz. can Italian-style
 plum tomatoes
1/2 cup dry white wine
2 tablespoons tomato
 paste
1 teaspoon each rosemary,
 pepper, basil, oregano
6 ruffled lasagne noodles

Bechamel Sauce:
3 tablespoons flour
1 1/4 cups skim milk
1 garlic clove, minced
pinch nutmeg
pinch of pepper
6 tablespoons fresh grated
 Parmesan cheese

SERVES 4

Char peppers in broiler, turning frequently. Place in paper bag 10 minutes, then peel off skins. Seed peppers and cut into 2" strips.

In a large saucepan, sauté onion and garlic in oil. Chop plum tomatoes and add to saucepan with their juice, wine, tomato paste and spices. Simmer until liquid is reduced by half.

Boil noodles until tender but firm to the bite. Drain, spread on towels and pat dry. Cut into 8-inch lengths, reserving ends.

Sauce: In a saucepan, blend flour and 1/4 cup milk. Whisk in remaining milk and spices. Stirring constantly, simmer for 2 minutes. Remove from heat, stir in Parmesan cheese.

Spray 8" x 8" pan with non-stick oil. Make 3 layers as follows: tomato sauce, 2 noodles and ends, bechamel sauce, and peppers. Dot top with bechamel. Bake at 400° for 30 minutes.

Serving: 1/4 Recipe	Calories: 381	Protein: 17 gm
Calories from Fat: 59	Total Fat: 7 gm	Dietary Fiber: 7 gm
Saturated Fat: 2 gm	Carbs: 59 gm	Sodium: 528 mg
Component of Fat: 15%	Cholesterol: 9 mg	Calcium: 303 mg

Cape Ann Tuna Casserole

1 lb. dry egg noodles
8 cups skim milk
$^1/_2$ tablespoon canola oil
$^1/_2$ cup chopped onion
2 cloves garlic, minced
$1^1/_2$ cups sliced mushrooms
1 teaspoon tamari or soy
    sauce
1 teaspoon black pepper
1 cup low-fat sour cream
2 eggs, beaten
1 cup grated part-skim
    mozzarella cheese
3-6 oz. cans tuna in water
1 cup cooked peas

SERVES 8

Heat milk until gently simmering. Add noodles and cook until tender, but firm to the bite. Drain, reserving 2 cups of the milk.

Sauté onion and garlic in oil. Add mushrooms, cover pan. When mushrooms begin to soften, add reserved milk, tamari or soy sauce, and pepper. Remove from heat, stir in sour cream, eggs and mozzarella. Drain tuna, flake into small pieces, and stir into mixture. Gently fold in peas and noodles.

Spray casserole with non-stick oil. Transfer mixture into casserole. Bake in preheated 350° oven for 25 minutes.

Serving: 1/8 Recipe
Calories from Fat: 61
Saturated Fat: 2 gm
Component of Fat: 14%

Calories: 425
Total Fat: 7 gm
Carbs: 55 gm
Cholesterol: 134 mg

Protein: 34 gm
Dietary Fiber: 3 gm
Sodium: 393 mg
Calcium: 225 mg

Layered Lobster Provençal

SERVES 8

Cheese Sauce:
3 tablespoons flour
1½ cups skim milk
2 egg yolks, beaten
pinch of nutmeg
salt and pepper to taste
⅔ cup grated low-fat
    Swiss Lorraine cheese

Fillings:
2 cups cooked lobster
    meat
2 tablespoons canola oil
3 tablespoons shallots
salt and pepper to taste
¼ cup dry vermouth
2 cups broccoli florets
3 cups sliced mushrooms
2 tablespoons lemon juice
1½ cups prepared tomato
    sauce

4 cups cooked rice

In a saucepan, slowly whisk milk into flour until smooth. Set over moderate heat and beat until sauce is smooth and thick. Remove from heat and briskly beat in egg yolks, nutmeg, salt and pepper. Stir in cheese.

Lobster: Briefly sauté lobster in oil with shallots, salt and pepper. Add vermouth and rapidly boil it down until just a little liquid remains. Fold in ½ cup cheese sauce. Broccoli: Briefly steam broccoli. Drain, and mix with ½ cup cheese sauce. Mushrooms: Simmer mushrooms and lemon juice in a covered pan 2 minutes. Remove lid, rapidly boil down. Fold in remaining cheese sauce.

In a large pan layer a thin coat tomato sauce, followed by layers of 2 cups rice, lobster meat, ¾ cup tomato sauce, broccoli, 2 cups rice, mushrooms then remaining tomato sauce. Bake in 350° oven 25 minutes.

Serving: 1/8 Recipe	Calories: 255	Protein: 14 gm
Calories from Fat: 42	Total Fat: 5 gm	Dietary Fiber: 2 gm
Saturated Fat: 1 gm	Carbs: 38 gm	Sodium: 443 mg
Component of Fat: 16%	Cholesterol: 31 mg	Calcium: 182 mg

Zucchini Risotto

1 medium onion, diced
2 tablespoons olive oil
$^1/_2$ cup chopped celery
2 cloves garlic, minced
2 cups dry aborio rice
$^1/_2$ cup dry white wine
1$^1/_2$ tablespoons tamari or
   soy sauce
6 cups boiling water
2 cups zucchini, diced
1 cup red pepper, diced
1 teasspoon saffron
1 tablespoon parsley
2 tesspoons butter
1 teaspoon black pepper
$^1/_3$ cup fresh grated
   Parmesan cheese

SERVES 6

In a large saucepan, sauté onion in oil. Add celery and garlic, cook until onion is clear. Stir in rice, then turn heat to high and add white wine. Cook until liquid is reduced by half. Reduce heat to medium.

In a separate pot, mix tamari or soy sauce into 6 cups boiling water. Add hot broth to risotto, $^1/_2$-cup at a time. Stir, and allow rice to absorb liquid after each addition. After final addition of broth, some liquid will remain. Add vegetables and spices. Cook 15 minutes more, adding liquid if needed. When rice is soft and creamy, stir in butter, pepper and Parmesan.

Serving: 1/6 Recipe	Calories: 408	Protein: 9 gm
Calories from Fat: 69	Total Fat: 8 gm	Dietary Fiber: 4 gm
Saturated Fat: 2.5 gm	Carbs: 69 gm	Sodium: 395 mg
Component of Fat: 17%	Cholesterol: 8 mg	Calcium: 113 mg

Chestnut Stuffing

Stuffing does not need to be "stuffed" to make a good side-dish.
This stuffing, however, is excellent for stuffing baked fish or shrimp.

1/2 lb. fresh chestnuts
1 tablespoon canola oil
1 cup chopped onion
1/2 cup chopped celery
1 teaspoon thyme
1 teaspoon sage
1 tablespoon parsley
salt and pepper to taste
2 cups stale French or
    plain toasting bread,
    cut into 1/3-inch cubes
1 cup warm skim milk
1 teaspoon finely grated
    lemon peel

SERVES 4

With a sharp paring knife, score an "X" in bottom of chestnuts. Place on cookie sheet in 350° oven and roast until shells are noticeably browned. When cool enough to handle, crack open and chop nut meats.

Sauté chestnuts, onion and celery in oil. Stir in spices, then bread cubes. Heat until bread cubes start to brown, then slowly pour in milk. Remove from heat and toss in lemon zest. Serve immediately or use for stuffing.

Serving: 1/4 Recipe	Calories: 262	Protein: 7 gm
Calories from Fat: 45	Total Fat: 5 gm	Dietary Fiber: 6 gm
Saturated Fat: 1 gm	Carbs: 48 gm	Sodium: 203 mg
Component of Fat: 17%	Cholesterol: 1 mg	Calcium: 134 mg

Rye Berries with Mushrooms

SERVES 4

1 cup rye berries
3 cups water
1 teaspoon safflower oil
2 tablespoons chopped
    shallots
1/2 cup chopped
    mushrooms
1 teaspoon basil
1 teaspoon sage
1 teaspoon parsley
salt and pepper to taste

Wash rye berries. In a covered pot, boil berries in water for 2 hours, or until tender.

Sauté shallots in oil. When almost clear, add mushrooms and spices. Cover pan, and turn heat to low. Leave on heat 10 minutes.

When rye berries have absorbed all the water and are soft, combine with sauté. Serve hot.

Serving: 1/4 Recipe	Calories: 43	Protein: 1 gm
Calories from Fat: 12	Total Fat: 1 gm	Dietary Fiber: 1 gm
Saturated Fat: 0 gm	Carbs: 7 gm	Sodium: 36 mg
Component of Fat: 26%	Cholesterol: 0 mg	Calcium: 19 mg

In New England's early years of shipbuilding, sloops and ketches were thought the ideal ships to serve the New England trade routes. Around 1720, the ketch began to give way to the schooner, which to this day is a very common sailing ship in these waters. Eventually, brigs weighing 100- 300 tons came to dominate the trade routes to Europe.

Maple Sugar Baked Beans

1 lb. pinto beans
1 teaspoon olive oil
2 cups chopped onion
1 clove minced garlic
2 tablespoons fresh
    grated ginger
2 cups apple cider
2 cups water
1 cup maple syrup
$1/_4$ cup brown sugar
1 tablespoon dry mustard
2 bay leaves
pinch of allspice
pinch of cloves
salt and pepper to taste

SERVES 6

Clean twigs and stones from beans, wash and soak overnight in cold water. The next morning, drain beans and rinse.

Heat olive oil in saucepan. Sauté onion, garlic and ginger until lightly browned. Combine beans, onion sauté, and remaining ingredients. Spray a large casserole or bean pot with non-stick oil, transfer mixture into prepared baking dish, and cover.

Bake in 350° oven 3 hours, or until tender, adding water as needed. Just before beans are finished, remove lid and brown.

Serving: 1/6 Recipe	Calories: 498	Protein: 17 gm
Calories from Fat: 21	Total Fat: 2 gm	Dietary Fiber: 1 gm
Saturated Fat: 0.5 gm	Carbs: 107 gm	Sodium: 41 mg
Component of Fat: 4%	Cholesterol: 0 mg	Calcium: 178 mg

Bean-Hole Beans

Norway, Maine has a Bean-Hole Bean Festival each July, celebrating this old New England dish.

2 lbs. dry beans
1 gallon water
$^1/_2$ cup molasses
$^1/_2$ cup brown sugar
3 tablespoons spiced
    prepared mustard
salt and pepper to taste

SERVES 12

Select large cast-iron pot with tight-fitting lid. Build an outdoor fire in a 2-foot square hole, preferably in gravel-type soil.

When fire has burned to hot coals, put beans and water in pot, and place on coals. Let the water boil for 5 minutes, then stir in molasses, brown sugar, mustard, salt and pepper. Place lid on pot. Remove some coals with a shovel, and place them on top of and around, the pot. Fill hole in with gravel or soil. Leave covered 6 hours, then dig up your bean-hole beans!

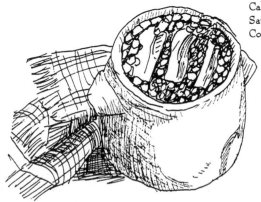

Serving: 1/12 Recipe	Calories: 121	Protein: 3 gm
Calories from Fat: 2	Total Fat: 0.5 gm	Dietary Fiber: 2 gm
Saturated Fat: 0 gm	Carbs: 27 gm	Sodium: 269 mg
Component of Fat: 2%	Cholesterol: 0 mg	Calcium: 74 mg

Savory Succotash

2 cups cooked lima beans
   (from dried or frozen)
2 cups fresh or frozen
   corn kernels
$^2/_3$ cup skim milk
$^1/_3$ cup non-fat powdered
   milk
1 tablespoon butter
1 clove garlic, minced
2 tablespoons finely
   chopped onion
1 teaspoon basil
1 teaspoon thyme
1 teaspoon black pepper
salt to taste

SERVES 6

If lima beans are dried, soak overnight, then add to boiling water and simmer 1 hour, or until tender. If lima beans are frozen, heat in boiling water 10 minutes.

Drain lima beans and return to pot. Add corn. Dissolve powdered milk in skim milk, and add to succotash with remaining ingredients. Simmer 20 minutes, but do not boil.

Serving: 1/6 Recipe
Calories from Fat: 21
Saturated Fat: 1 gm
Component of Fat: 12%

Calories: 160
Total Fat: 2 gm
Carbs: 28 gm
Cholesterol: 6 mg

Protein: 9 gm
Dietary Fiber: 5 gm
Sodium: 76 mg
Calcium: 103 mg

In New England, the Native Indians planted corn, beans and squash together on a mound, and these were eaten together as well. In Iroquois myth, they represented three inseparable sisters. The corn grew straight and tall, the beans climbed the corn, and the squash plant trailed down the mounds and covered the ground with fruit.

Vegetables
and
Sauces

CONTENTS

Carrot-Beet Julienne

$^1/_2$ cup water

2 cups carrots, peeled
   and cut diagonally
   into thin strips

2 cups beets, peeled and
   cut diagonally into
   thin strips

1 teaspoon butter

1 tablespoon honey

2 tablespoons orange juice

1 teaspoon vinegar

pinch of salt

1 teaspoon lemon juice

$^1/_2$ teaspoon chopped
   parsley

SERVES 4

In a saucepan, boil water over medium-high heat. Add all ingredients, except parsley. Continue to cook until water evaporates, about 10 minutes.

Remove from heat, stir to coat vegetables. Sprinkle with parsley before serving.

Serving: 1/4 Recipe	Calories: 96	Protein: 2 gm
Calories from Fat: 11	Total Fat: 1 gm	Dietary Fiber: 6 gm
Saturated Fat: 1 gm	Carbs: 20 gm	Sodium: 145 mg
Component of Fat: 11%	Cholesterol: 3 mg	Calcium: 37 mg

Fresh Roasted Corn

freshly harvested corn in
   the husk
$1/2$ tablespoon butter
   for every 2 ears
1 teaspoon salt

EARS PER PERSON

Pull down corn husks just far enough to remove silk. After removing silk, run water into corn ear, drain, then close up husk and twist shut.

Roast ears over hot coals, or in 400° oven, for 20 minutes or until kernels are tender, while occasionally turning ears over.

In a tall pot, heat water, butter and salt. Pull back husk and dangle ear from husk. Dip ear in hot buttered water and a thin film of butter will coat the corn. Allow excess water and butter to drip back into the pot.

Serving: 2 Ears	Calories: 44	Protein: 1 gm
Calories from Fat: 7	Total Fat: 1 gm	Dietary Fiber: 1 gm
Saturated Fat: 0 gm	Carbs: 10 gm	Sodium: 36 mg
Component of Fat: 13%	Cholesterol: 1 mg	Calcium: 1 mg

Indian Peas

2 tablespoons chopped
   onion
1 teaspoon safflower oil
2 cups shelled peas, raw or
   very lightly steamed
$^2/_3$ cup cornmeal
2 cups skim milk
1 egg, beaten
pinch of salt
pinch of pepper
2 tablespoons parsley

SERVES 4

Preheat oven to 350°. Spray a $1^1/_2$-quart casserole with non-stick oil.

Sauté onion in oil until nearly clear. Place onion and peas in casserole. In a mixing bowl, combine cornmeal, milk, egg, salt and pepper. Blend well, and then pour over peas and onion. Sprinkle parsley over top. Bake 20-25 minutes, stirring occasionally.

Serving: 1/4 Recipe	Calories: 213	Protein: 12 gm
Calories from Fat: 31	Total Fat: 3.5 gm	Dietary Fiber: 6 gm
Saturated Fat: 1 gm	Carbs: 35 gm	Sodium: 120 mg
Component of Fat: 14%	Cholesterol: 56 mg	Calcium: 187 mg

One of the oldest methods of Native American cookery was baking, or frying, on a flat stone that had been heated over an open fire. Not only was bread baked in this fashion, but cornmeal was often mixed with vegetables or fish and baked together on a stone. The Indians of this region used corn as an integral part of every meal.

Chilled Green Beans

1 lb. fresh green beans
3 tablespoons finely
    chopped onion
1 clove minced garlic
1 tablespoon olive oil
2 tablespoons wine
    vinegar
1 teaspoon lemon juice
3 tablespoons diced
    pimentos
1/2 teaspoon pepper
salt to taste
2 tablespoons grated
    Parmesan cheese

SERVES 6

Wash and clean green beans, snapping off ends and tough filament that pulls off with the tips of larger beans. Place on vegetable steamer over boiling water, cover and steam until tender. Remove and drain.

Combine remaining ingredients, except the Parmesan cheese, and pour over green beans. Toss and chill. Just before serving, sprinkle with grated Parmesan.

Serving: 1/6 Recipe
Calories from Fat: 27
Saturated Fat: 1 gm
Component of Fat: 42%

Calories: 60
Total Fat: 3 gm
Carbs: 7 gm
Cholesterol: 1 mg

Protein: 2 gm
Dietary Fiber: 3 gm
Sodium: 67 mg
Calcium: 62 mg

Baked Tomatoes
with Yellow Squash Stuffing

4 large beefsteak-type
    tomatoes
2 teaspoons canola oil
2 tablespoons chopped
    scallions
$^1/_2$ cup finely chopped
    celery
1 clove crushed garlic
1 cup finely chopped
    yellow squash
2 tablespoons fresh, finely
    chopped parsley
pinch of salt
$^1/_2$ teaspoon black pepper
$^1/_2$ cup plain bread
    crumbs

SERVES 4

Preheat oven to 350°. Cut large hollows in the stem end of tomatoes, being careful not to cut through the bottoms. Scoop out most of the seeds and pulp. Invert tomatoes on a rack, and drain 15 minutes.

Sauté scallion, celery and garlic in oil. Add yellow squash, cover pan and cook 5 minutes. Drain off liquid, add spices and bread crumbs. Fill tomatoes with stuffing.

Select a baking pan in which the tomatoes can be tightly placed, side-by-side. Spray pan with non-stick oil and pour in $^1/_2$-cup water. Arrange tomatoes in pan. Bake 10-15 minutes, then remove with slotted spoon.

Serving: 1/4 Recipe	Calories: 75	Protein: 2 gm
Calories from Fat: 27	Total Fat: 3 gm	Dietary Fiber: 3 gm
Saturated Fat: 0.5 gm	Carbs: 11 gm	Sodium: 100 mg
Component of Fat: 33%	Cholesterol: 0 mg	Calcium: 33 mg

Mushroom Quiche

2 tablespoons chopped
   onion
1 tablespoon canola oil
2 cups sliced mushrooms
2 whole eggs
1 egg, separated
1/2 lb. low-fat cottage
   cheese
1/2 teaspoon black pepper
pinch of salt
1/2 teaspoon paprika
2 tablespoons chopped
   fresh parsley

SERVES 6

Preheat oven to 375°. Spray a 9-inch pie pan with non-stick oil.

Sauté onion in oil until almost clear. Add mushrooms and cook 4 minutes more.

Beat eggs and egg yolk. In a separate bowl, lightly whip single egg white, then brush it over the bottom and sides of pie plate. Combine remaining egg white with other eggs. Mix in cottage cheese, sautéed onion, mushrooms and spices. Pour into pie plate and bake 15 minutes. Lower heat to 325° and bake 35 minutes more, or until quiche is firm and light brown.

Serving: 1/6 Recipe	Calories: 91	Protein: 8 gm
Calories from Fat: 45	Total Fat: 5 gm	Dietary Fiber: 0 gm
Saturated Fat: 1 gm	Carbs: 3 gm	Sodium: 207 mg
Component of Fat: 50%	Cholesterol: 109 mg	Calcium: 38 mg

Broccoli with Lemon Butter

1 large head broccoli
1 teaspoon butter
1 tablespoon olive oil
3 tablespoons white wine
1 tablespoon lemon juice
salt and pepper to taste

SERVES 4

Cut broccoli into spears, and place in steamer over boiling water. Broccoli is done when dark green and tender, about 7 minutes. Do not overcook.

While broccoli is cooking, melt butter with remaining ingredients in a very small saucepan. Drain broccoli. Pour lemon butter over broccoli florets. Serve immediately.

Serving: 1/4 Recipe	Calories: 69	Protein: 4 gm
Calories from Fat: 43	Total Fat: 5 gm	Dietary Fiber: 4 gm
Saturated Fat: 1 gm	Carbs: 3 gm	Sodium: 79 mg
Component of Fat: 55%	Cholesterol: 3 mg	Calcium: 49 mg

Quoddy Head, Maine, is the northern most point of the eastern United States. Estimates of the length of the Maine coast vary from 2,500 to 3,500 miles. The length depends on how it is measured around bays and promontories, and whether it is measured at high or low tide, which rises and falls 10 to 20 feet twice a day.

Herbed Cauliflower

1 clove minced garlic
2 teaspoons butter
1 head fresh cauliflower
2 stalks celery with
    leaves
$^1/_4$ cup white wine
$^1/_2$ cup skim milk
1 tablespoon chopped
    parsley
pinch of basil
pinch of rosemary
$^1/_2$ teaspoon pepper
$^1/_2$ cup grated low-fat
    Swiss Lorraine cheese

SERVES 4

In a medium-sized saucepan, sauté garlic in butter. Cut cauliflower into florets, and add to saucepan with celery stalks, white wine and milk. Cover, and gently steam 10 minutes. Remove cauliflower with slotted spoon. Add remaining spices to broth, but not the cheese. Leave uncovered and cook down until liquid is reduced by half. Remove celery stalks, and reduce heat to medium. Toss in cauliflower and cook 3-4 minutes longer. Serve cauliflower with sauce, covered with grated cheese.

Serving: 1/4 Recipe
Calories from Fat: 29
Saturated Fat: 2 gm
Component of Fat: 25%

Calories: 104
Total Fat: 3 gm
Carbs: 10 gm
Cholesterol: 10 mg

Protein: 10 gm
Dietary Fiber: 6 gm
Sodium: 162 mg
Calcium: 228 mg

Spicy Roasted Potatoes

16 small red potatoes
2 tablespoons Dijon
    mustard
1 egg white
2 tablespoons vinegar
1 tablespoon paprika
1 teaspoon cumin
pinch of garlic
pinch of cayenne
pinch of black pepper
pinch of salt

SERVES 4

Preheat oven to 400°. Spray a large oven pan with 3 coats non-stick oil. Scrub potatoes, and slice into $1/2$-inch thick rounds. Prick each round in 3-4 places with fork.

Whisk together remaining ingredients in large mixing bowl. Toss in potatoes, stir to coat. Soak potatoes in spices 15 minutes, stirring every few minutes.

Using a slotted spoon, remove potatoes and place in oven pan with some space between them. Roast in preheated oven 40 minutes, or until golden brown and tender.

Serving: 1/4 Recipe	Calories: 104	Protein: 5 gm
Calories from Fat: 9	Total Fat: 1 gm	Dietary Fiber: 3 gm
Saturated Fat: 0 gm	Carbs: 20 gm	Sodium: 91 mg
Component of Fat: 9%	Cholesterol: 0 mg	Calcium: 30 mg

123

Zucchini Hash Browns

3 cups grated zucchini
1 cup grated potatoes
2 tablespoons flour
1 tablespoon grated onion
1 tablespoon chopped
   parsley
1 teaspoon black pepper
pinch of salt
$1/2$ teaspoon garlic powder
2 teaspoons canola oil
2 egg whites, beaten
1 tablespoon canola oil for
   frying

SERVES 4

Cover a cotton kitchen towel with paper towels. Place grated zucchini on top of paper towels. Fold towels together, twist and wring moisture out of zucchini, then measure out 3 cups. In a large mixing bowl, toss zucchini and potatoes, sprinkle with flour. Stir in grated onion, parsley, and spices. Let mixture rest 15 minutes. Add 2 teaspoons canola oil and egg whites, stirring just enough to combine.

Spray large frying pan with non-stick oil. Pour in just enough oil to coat pan. Preheat pan on medium-high about 5 minutes, then fry hash browns until crispy on both sides.

Serving: 1/4 Recipe	Calories: 140	Protein: 5 gm
Calories from Fat: 54	Total Fat: 6 gm	Dietary Fiber: 3 gm
Saturated Fat: 0.5 gm	Carbs: 18 gm	Sodium: 66 mg
Component of Fat: 37%	Cholesterol: 0 mg	Calcium: 33 mg

Artichoke Florentine

SERVES 6

6 artichoke hearts,
   prepared as
   decribed below
1 lb. bag fresh spinach
¼ teaspoon nutmeg
salt and pepper to taste

Cream Sauce:
1 tablespoon butter
1 tablespoon flour
⅔ cup skim milk
1 egg yolk
¼ teaspoon white pepper
6 teaspoons grated cheese

Prepare artichoke hearts. Wash spinach, remove stems. Steam until just wilted, drain, chop and press out moisture. Combine spinach with spices. Place artichoke hearts in pan sprayed with non-stick oil. Spoon spinach into artichokes. Cover with Cream Sauce and grated cheese. Bake 10 minutes at 400°.

Cream Sauce: melt butter in saucepan, then blend in flour to make a roux. Whisk in milk, egg yolks and white pepper. Stirring constantly, cook until thickened. Pour sauce over artichoke hearts and sprinkle with grated cheese. This sauce works well on many vegetables.

Serving: 1/6 Recipe	Calories: 88	Protein: 6 gm
Calories from Fat: 32	Total Fat: 4 gm	Dietary Fiber: 4 gm
Saturated Fat: 2 gm	Carbs: 10 gm	Sodium: 194 mg
Component of Fat: 33%	Cholesterol: 43 mg	Calcium: 154 mg

To Prepare Artichoke Hearts: Slice off bottom stem, rub cut area with lemon. Keep chokes in bowl of vinegar-water when not working on them. To open artichoke center, push leaves apart, turn upside down on hard surface and press firmly on bottom. Remove fuzzy choke with spoon. Boil in water for 20 minutes. Pull off leaves, and heart will remain.

Mixed Steamed Greens

½ cup chopped onion
1 clove garlic, minced
1 tablespoon olive oil
¼ cup white wine
1 bay leaf
4 packed cups chopped
     mixed greens: mustard
     greens, kale, spinach,
     beet and collard greens
salt and pepper to taste

SERVES 4

In a large saucepan, sauté onion and garlic in olive oil and white wine for 4 minutes. Add bay leaf, then cover.

Wash and chop greens before firmly packing into measuring cups. Add greens to saucepan, cover and steam. Stir occasionally.

Cook until greens are as you like. I like them lightly steamed, but others prefer them completely cooked down. Less cooking retains more vitamins. When ready to serve, drain liquid and discard bay leaf.

Serving: 1/4 Recipe
Calories from Fat: 33
Saturated Fat: 0.5 gm
Component of Fat: 42%

Calories: 73
Total Fat: 4 gm
Carbs: 6 gm
Cholesterol: 0 mg

Protein: 3 gm
Dietary Fiber: 3 gm
Sodium: 139 mg
Calcium: 103 mg

Off the coast of New Hampshire are the Isles of Shoals, accessible by ferry. The islands have been praised by Whittier, Hawthorne and Longfellow. Chile Hassam illustrated an 1890's book by Celia Thaxter, daughter of a lighthouse keeper on Appledore, called *An Island Garden*. The magnificent garden on this Isle of Shoals has since been recreated.

Zucchini Frittata

1 teaspoon olive oil
3 cups sliced zucchini
2 tablespoons finely
    minced sun-dried
    tomatoes
$1/4$ cup finely chopped
    onion
1 cup corn kernels
3 eggs
3 egg whites
$1/2$ teaspoon black pepper
1 teaspoon dill
2 tablespoons grated low-
    fat Cheddar cheese
1 teaspoon paprika

SERVES 4

Preheat oven to 350°. Spray 8" x 11" glass or ceramic oven dish with non-stick oil.

In a large saucepan over medium heat, mix olive oil with zucchini, sun-dried tomatoes, onion and corn. Cover pan and steam vegetables for about 10 minutes.

In a large mixing bowl, whisk together eggs, whites, pepper and dill. Stir in steamed vegetables and cheese. Pour into oven dish and sprinkle with paprika. Bake 15 minutes, or until eggs are set up.

Serving: 1/4 Recipe	Calories: 151	Protein: 12 gm
Calories from Fat: 51	Total Fat: 6 gm	Dietary Fiber: 3 gm
Saturated Fat: 2 gm	Carbs: 15 gm	Sodium: 143 mg
Component of Fat: 32%	Cholesterol: 164 mg	Calcium: 115 mg

Quick Stir-Fry Asparagus

1 lb. fresh asparagus
2 teaspoons olive oil
2 tablespoons white wine
$\frac{1}{4}$ teaspoon black pepper
2 tablespoons grated
   Romano cheese

SERVES 4

Cut base of stalks off asparagus. If asparagus are thick, scrape skin off lower ends of stalks. Spray large saucepan with non-stick oil. Heat olive oil in pan over medium heat. Place asparagus in hot oil (keeping stalks parallel will maintain their good looks). Pour in white wine. Cover pan and cook 3 minutes. Uncover, toss lightly, add more white wine if drying out. When asparagus are just barely tender, they are done. Sprinkle with black pepper. Place in serving dish, and lightly toss with Romano cheese.

Serving: 1/4 Recipe	Calories: 71	Protein: 5 gm
Calories from Fat: 39	Total Fat: 4 gm	Dietary Fiber: 1 gm
Saturated Fat: 1 gm	Carbs: 2 gm	Sodium: 75 mg
Component of Fat: 54%	Cholesterol: 5 mg	Calcium: 68 mg

COASTAL NEW ENGLAND   SUMMERTIME COOKING

Rutabaga Mash

2 lbs. rutabagas
1 tablespoon butter
³/₄ cup non-fat plain
    yogurt
salt and pepper to taste

SERVES 6

Scrub and peel rutabagas. Dice into ¹/₂-inch cubes. Steam 20 minutes, or until tender. Drain off water.

Transfer rutabagas into large bowl, melt butter over hot rutabagas, then add yogurt, salt and pepper. Mash with potato masher.

Serving: 1/6 Recipe	Calories: 81	Protein: 3 gm
Calories from Fat: 20	Total Fat: 2 gm	Dietary Fiber: 0 gm
Saturated Fat: 1 gm	Carbs: 13 gm	Sodium: 86 mg
Component of Fat: 23%	Cholesterol: 6 mg	Calcium: 111 mg

In 1524, the Frenchman Giovanni da Verrazano mapped the southern New England coastline north to Cape Cod. In the following year, a Portuguese sailor, Estevan Gomez, sailing under the Spanish flag, mapped the remaining New England coastline and farther north, into what is today the maritimes of New Brunswick.

Onion Pie Au Gratin

1 egg white
2 cups chopped onion or
    shallots
2 teaspoons canola oil
3 eggs, beaten
1 cup skim milk
$\frac{1}{4}$ cup non-fat dry
    powdered milk
1 teaspoon Worcestershire
    sauce
$\frac{1}{2}$ cup grated fresh
    Parmesan cheese

SERVES 6

Preheat oven to 375°. Spray a 9-inch pie plate with non-stick oil. Lightly beat egg white, then brush over the bottom and sides of the pie plate.

Sauté onion or shallots in oil until nearly clear. In a mixing bowl, beat together eggs, milks and Worcestershire sauce. Stir in grated cheese and sautéed onions or shallots. Pour into pie plate. Bake 30 minutes or until golden brown.

Serving: 1/6 Recipe
Calories from Fat: 53
Saturated Fat: 2 gm
Component of Fat: 42%

Calories: 127
Total Fat: 6 gm
Carbs: 9 gm
Cholesterol: 114 mg

Protein: 9 gm
Dietary Fiber: 1 gm
Sodium: 212 mg
Calcium: 199 mg

Desserts
and
Sweets

CONTENTS

Note: The nutritional analysis for pies is based on 8 pieces per pie.

Strawberry Crisp

SERVES 8

4 cups strawberries,
    hulled and halved
3 tablespoons cornstarch
$1/_2$ cup sugar
1 tablespoon lemon juice
1 teaspoon vanilla extract
$1/_3$ cup all-purpose flour
1 cup rolled oats
$1/_2$ cup brown sugar
$1/_2$ teaspoon nutmeg
pinch of salt
2 tablespoons butter,
    melted
1 egg, beaten

Preheat oven to 350°. Spray 9-inch square baking dish with non-stick oil.

Toss strawberries with cornstarch, sugar, lemon juice and vanilla. Place in baking dish.

Mix flour, oats, brown sugar, nutmeg and salt. Sprinkle with butter, then use fork to distribute evenly. Stir in egg. Spread over strawberries. Bake about 25 minutes or until lightly browned.

Serving: 1/8 Recipe	Calories: 229	Protein: 3 gm
Calories from Fat: 40	Total Fat: 4 gm	Dietary Fiber: 2 gm
Saturated Fat: 2 gm	Carbs: 45 gm	Sodium: 59 mg
	Cholesterol: 35 mg	Calcium: 32 mg

Peach Crumb Cobbler

Peach Filling:
6 cups fresh peeled peach
    slices
$\frac{1}{2}$ cup sugar
3 tablespoons cornstarch
2 tablespoons white wine
2 teaspoons lemon juice
1 teaspoon fresh mint,
    chopped very fine

Topping:
$\frac{1}{2}$ cup all-purpose flour
$\frac{1}{2}$ cup light brown sugar
2 teaspoons cinnamon
2 tablespoons butter,
    softened

SERVES 8

Preheat oven to 350°. Spray 9-inch deep-dish pie plate with non-stick oil.

Peach Filling: In a mixing bowl, combine peaches, sugar and cornstarch. Toss to coat peaches. Add wine, lemon juice and mint, then mix. Pour into deep-dish pie plate.

Topping: Mix flour with brown sugar and cinnamon. Using pastry cutter or two knives, cut in butter until mixture resembles coarse crumbs. Sprinkle over peaches. Bake 45 minutes. Serve warm or cold. Cobbler is especially good with frozen yogurt on top!

Serving: 1/8 Recipe	Calories: 212	Protein: 2 gm
Calories from Fat: 28	Total Fat: 3 gm	Dietary Fiber: 3 gm
Saturated Fat: 2 gm	Carbs: 46 gm	Sodium: 36 mg
Component of Fat: 12%	Cholesterol: 8 mg	Calcium: 27 mg

The National Seashore is the preserving force of the Cape Cod coast. The National Park Service, U.S. Fish and Wildlife Service, Nature Conservancy and Audubon Societies also contribute efforts and resources to protect these sensitive coastal wetlands and the delicate balance of plant, animal and bird life, with the wants and needs of people. (cont.)

Raspberry Pie

MAKES 9-INCH PIE

Crust:
2¹/₂ cups all-purpose flour
3 tablespoons sugar
6 tablespoons canola oil
7 tablespoons ice water
1 tablespoon skim milk

Raspberry Filling:
4 cups fresh raspberries
1 teaspoon vanilla extract
²/₃ cup sugar
3 tablespoons cornstarch

Glaze:
1 tablespoon skim milk
1 tablespoon sugar

Preheat oven to 350°. Spray 9-inch pie plate with non-stick oil. Combine flour and sugar. With pastry cutter or knives, cut oil into mixture. Blend in water and milk. Divide dough in half and roll each between sheets of wax paper. Place bottom crust in pie plate.

Sprinkle raspberries with vanilla, then sugar and cornstarch. Let mixture set for 30 minutes. Transfer into pie shell. Cover with top crust, crimp and flute edges. Make 5 small slits in top, brush with milk and sprinkle with sugar. Bake 40 minutes.

Serving: 1 Piece	Calories: 365	Protein: 5 gm
Calories from Fat: 99	Total Fat: 11 gm	Dietary Fiber: 5 gm
Saturated Fat: 1 gm	Carbs: 63 gm	Sodium: 4 mg
Component of Fat: 27%	Cholesterol: 0 mg	Calcium: 25 mg

(cont.) When Henry David Thoreau travelled these shores in 1849, he described the journey in his book, *Cape Cod*. But shifting sands and tidal action have since moved part of his walking path over 400 feet out to sea! By providing educational awareness, the National Seashore preserves the shore for our enjoyment and the well-being of wildlife.

Maine Wild Blueberry Pie

Crust:
2$\frac{1}{2}$ cups all-purpose flour
3 tablespoons sugar
6 tablespoons canola oil
7 tablespoons ice water
1 tablespoon skim milk

Blueberry Filling:
4 cups wild blueberries
$\frac{1}{3}$ cup sugar
$\frac{1}{3}$ cup brown sugar
1 tablespoon quick tapioca
$\frac{1}{2}$ teaspoon cinnamon
$\frac{1}{2}$ teaspoon nutmeg
1 tablespoon lemon juice

Glaze:
1 tablespoon skim milk
1 tablespoon sugar

MAKES 9-INCH PIE

Preheat oven to 400°. Spray 9-inch pie plate with non-stick oil.

Crust: Combine flour and sugar. With pastry cutter or knives, cut oil into mixture. Use fork to blend in water and milk. Divide dough in half, and roll each between two sheets of wax paper. Place bottom crust in pie plate.

Clean fresh blueberries (if canned or frozen set to drain) and put in bowl. In a separate bowl, mix sugars, tapioca, cinnamon and nutmeg. Sprinkle lemon juice on blueberries, then gently fold into sugar mixture. Let sit 45 minutes, then gently stir again. Pour into pie shell. Cover with second crust. Crimp edges with fingers and flute. Make 5 small slits in top. Brush top with milk and sprinkle with sugar. Bake 10 minutes at 400°, reduce heat to 350° and bake 25 minutes more.

Serving: 1 Piece	Calories: 371	Protein: 5 gm
Calories from Fat: 98	Total Fat: 11 gm	Dietary Fiber: 3 gm
Saturated Fat: 1 gm	Carbs: 65 gm	Sodium: 11 mg
Component of Fat: 26%	Cholesterol: 0 mg	Calcium: 25 mg

Apple Kuchen with Almond Topping

Crust and Fruit: SERVES 12
1¼ cups flour
¼ cup sugar
½ teaspoon baking
    powder
6 tablespoons canola oil
1 egg
2¼ cups peeled and finely
    diced apples

Topping:
8 oz. non-fat cream cheese
½ cup confectioner's
    sugar
¼ cup brown sugar
½ teaspoon almond
    extract
2 eggs
¼ cup skim milk
³⁄₈ cup all-purpose flour
1 teaspoon baking powder
5 tablspoons almond
    slivers

Preheat oven to 350°. Spray 9" x 12" pan with non-stick oil.

Crust and Fruit: Combine flour, sugar and baking powder. Work in oil with fingertips or pastry cutter. Quickly blend in egg. Distribute the dough in dabs over the bottom of pan. Freeze 15 minutes. Flour fingertips and press dough over bottom and up sides. Spread apples over dough. Bake 15 minutes.

Topping: With electric beater, combine cream cheese, sugars and almond extract until fluffy. Add eggs and milk. In a separate bowl, sift flour and baking powder, then add almond slivers. Briefly stir flour mixture into cream cheese mixture.

When crust and apples have baked 15 minutes, spread prepared topping over apples, and bake for another 25 minutes.

Serving: 1/12 Recipe	Calories: 246	Protein: 7 gm
Calories from Fat: 91	Total Fat: 10 gm	Dietary Fiber: 2 gm
Saturated Fat: 1 gm	Carbs: 32 gm	Sodium: 185 mg
Component of Fat: 37%	Cholesterol: 54 mg	Calcium: 115 mg

Blackberry Clafouti

Blackberries grow wild all over coastal New England, the wooded shoreline has so many that local berry lovers aren't able to eat them all!

2 cups fresh blackberries
$^3/_4$ cup non-fat plain
    yogurt
$^3/_4$ cup non-fat cottage
    cheese
$^1/_2$ cup skim milk
1 egg
$^1/_2$ teaspoon lemon juice
$^1/_4$ cup all-purpose flour
$^1/_2$ teaspoon vanilla extract
6 tablespoons sugar
pinch of cinnamon

SERVES 4

Preheat oven to 425°. Spray 4 custard cups with non-stick oil. Spread blackberries in bottom of cups.

In a blender, whip together yogurt and cottage cheese until smooth. Add remaining ingredients and process again.

Pour custard over berries in cups. Bake 25 minutes, or until lightly golden on top.

Serve warm in custard cups or run a butter knife around the edges and invert onto serving plates.

Serving: 1/4 Recipe	Calories: 218	Protein: 11 gm
Calories from Fat: 14	Total Fat: 2 gm	Dietary Fiber: 4 gm
Saturated Fat: 0 gm	Carbs: 41 gm	Sodium: 223 mg
Component of Fat: 6%	Cholesterol: 55 mg	Calcium: 160 mg

Chocolate Boston Cream Pie

Cake Batter:
4 tablespoons unsalted
   butter, softened
$2^1/_2$ cups sifted cake flour
1 tablespoon baking
   powder
$^1/_2$ teaspoon salt
$1^3/_4$ cups sugar
$^1/_2$ cup unsweetened cocoa
   powder
1 cup skim milk
1 teaspoon vanilla extract
2 eggs
2 egg whites

Cream Filling:
$^1/_2$ cup sugar
2 tablespoons cornstarch
$1^1/_2$ cups skim milk
1 egg
3 tablespoons cocoa
   powder
1 teaspoon vanilla extract

Top with 2 tablespoons
   powdered sugar

MAKES 9-INCH CAKE

Preheat oven to 350°. Spray two 9-inch round layer-cake pans with non-stick oil.

In a large mixing bowl, use electric beater to blend cake batter ingredients. Beat 3 minutes on high speed, then pour into pans. Bake 30 minutes, or until toothpick inserted in cakes comes out clean. Cool in pan for 10 minutes, then turn onto wire rack and cool thoroughly.

In a saucepan, mix sugar, cornstarch, milk, egg and cocoa. Stirring constantly, cook over medium heat until mixture boils. Let boil one minute. Remove from heat and stir in vanilla. Cool to room temperature before layering.

Spread cream filling between cake layers. Sprinkle the top with powdered sugar.

Serving: 1 Piece	Calories: 499	Protein: 10 gm
Calories from Fat: 80	Total Fat: 9 gm	Dietary Fiber: 2 gm
Saturated Fat: 5 gm	Carbs: 95 gm	Sodium: 379 mg
Component of Fat: 16%	Cholesterol: 98 mg	Calcium: 181 mg

Grape Sorbet

1 lb. grapes, any kind
   or color
1/2 cup apple juice
1/4 cup sugar

SERVES 4

Process grapes in blender. Strain grape skins and seeds from purée.

Combine apple juice with sugar in a saucepan. Stir over low heat until sugar is dissolved. Remove from heat, mix in grape purée.

Pour into 8-inch square pan and set in freezer. Using rubber spatula, stir every 15 minutes until creamy, about 2 hours. Cover and allow to freeze. To serve, scoop into small dishes, garnish with mint, if desired.

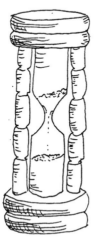

Serving: 1/4 Recipe	Calories: 135	Protein: 1 gm
Calories from Fat: 4	Total Fat: 0.5 gm	Dietary Fiber: 1 gm
Saturated Fat: 0 gm	Carbs: 36 gm	Sodium: 3 mg
Component of Fat: 3%	Cholesterol: 0 mg	Calcium: 18 mg

Portsmouth Pear Spice Cake

Hardy pears grow well throughout all of New England, especially the more temperate coastal areas. This pear cake is moist and delicious!

1½ cups packed brown sugar

4 tablespoons unsalted butter, softened

1 cup applesauce

1 teaspoon vanilla

2 teaspoons baking powder

½ teaspoon baking soda

2 teaspoons cinnamon

1 teaspoon ginger

1 teaspoon cloves

2½ cups all-purpose flour

3 eggs

3 medium-size ripe pears

¼ cup chopped almonds

Frosting:

2 tablespoons skim milk

8 oz. non-fat cream cheese

1 teaspoon vanilla

2½ cups powdered sugar

SERVES 12

Preheat oven to 350°. Spray a 9" x 13" baking pan with non-stick oil.

With electric beater, combine sugar, butter, applesauce, vanilla, baking powder, baking soda, cinnamon, ginger, cloves, salt and flour. Beat at medium-high speed 5 minutes. Add eggs, beating after each one.

Peel pears and chop into very small pieces. With a rubber spatula, fold pears and nuts into batter. Spread batter in baking pan. Bake 50 minutes, or until toothpick inserted in center comes out clean. Remove cake from pan, and cool on wire rack before frosting.

Frosting: Combine milk, cream cheese and vanilla with electric beater until fluffy. Slowly add sugar until frosting is of spreading consistency. Frost when cake is cool.

Serving: 1 Piece	Calories: 353	Protein: 8 gm
Calories from Fat: 64	Total Fat: 7 gm	Dietary Fiber: 7 gm
Saturated Fat: 3 gm	Carbs: 65 gm	Sodium: 256 mg
Component of Fat: 18%	Cholesterol: 65 mg	Calcium: 133 mg

Maple-Hazelnut Torte
with Maple Sugar Icing

6 eggs, separated
1 cup sugar
$\frac{1}{2}$ cup bread crumbs,
   (coarse, not fine)
$\frac{1}{4}$ cup unsweetened
   grated chocolate
$\frac{1}{2}$ cup coarsely ground
   hazelnuts
2 tablespoons maple
   syrup
1 teaspoon vanilla extract
$\frac{1}{2}$ teaspoon double-acting
   baking powder
$\frac{1}{2}$ teaspoon cinnamon

Maple Sugar Icing:
2 cups powdered sugar
1 tablespoon skim milk
$\frac{1}{2}$ teaspoon vanilla
$\frac{1}{2}$ cup maple syrup
   (more or less)

SERVES 10

Preheat oven to 325°. Have all ingredients at room temperature. Beat egg yolks until light and lemon-colored. Sift sugar and gradually beat it into the yolks. Add all other ingredients except the egg whites.

In separate bowl, beat egg whites until stiff. Gently fold into batter. Pour batter into ungreased 9-inch spring-form or tube pan, so cake can be removed without much handling. Bake 1 hour. Cool completely before icing.

Maple Sugar Icing: Sift powdered sugar. Blend in milk and vanilla. Stir in maple syrup to desired consistency (thicker if spreading on cake, thinner if pouring over individual pieces.)

Serving: 1 Piece
Calories from Fat: 82
Saturated Fat: 2 gm
Component of Fat: 24%

Calories: 333
Total Fat: 9 gm
Carbs: 61 gm
Cholesterol: 129 mg

Protein: 5 gm
Dietary Fiber: 1 gm
Sodium: 128 mg
Calcium: 72 mg

Chocolate-Pecan Oatmeal Cookies

(Although reduced in fat, eating these cookies by the dozen does not follow the guidelines of the American Heart Association!)

4 tablespoons unsalted
    butter, softened
$1/_2$ cup brown sugar
$1/_2$ cup granulated sugar
1 egg
2 egg whites
1 teaspoon vanilla extract
$1/_4$ cup apple juice
    concentrate
1 cup all-purpose flour
$1/_2$ teaspoon baking soda
$1/_2$ teaspoon double-acting
    baking powder
1 cup uncooked quick
    rolled oats
$1/_2$ cup mini chocolate
    chips
$1/_4$ cup chopped pecans

MAKES 4 DOZEN COOKIES

Preheat oven to 350°. Spray cookie sheet with non-stick oil.

Cream together butter and sugars. Beat in egg, whites, vanilla and apple juice concentrate.

In a separate bowl, sift together flour, baking soda and baking powder. Beat into the wet mixture. When smooth, mix in rolled oats, then chocolate chips and nuts. Drop batter by heaping teaspoons, 2 inches apart, on cookie sheet. Bake 10-12 minutes or until cookie bottoms are light brown.

Serving: 1 Cookie	Calories: 45	Protein: 1 gm
Calories from Fat: 18	Total Fat: 2 gm	Dietary Fiber: 0 gm
Saturated Fat: 1 gm	Carbs: 6 gm	Sodium: 27 mg
Component of Fat: 40%	Cholesterol: 12 mg	Calcium: 7 mg

Along the eastern shore of Newport, Rhode Island, is a three-mile path known as Cliff Walk, running between the grand old summer mansions (the first of the New England shingle-style "Cottages") and the sea. Cliff Walk is a public way, and the courts have affirmed it as "the vested right of the humblest citizen of Newport in the Atlantic Ocean."

A Summer's Night Chocolate Kisses

Like a summer's night kisses, these will disappear too soon!

4 egg whites
pinch of salt
$\frac{1}{4}$ teaspoon cream of
    tartar
$\frac{1}{3}$ cup granulated sugar
$\frac{1}{2}$ cup confectioner's
    sugar
3 tablespoons cocoa
    powder

MAKES 3 DOZEN 1-INCH MERINGUES

Preheat oven to 200°. Spray cookie sheet with non-stick oil.

Beat egg whites with salt and cream of tartar until foamy. Slowly beat in granulated sugar, 1 tablespoon at a time (the meringue should become stiff.) Using a spatula, gently fold in confectioner's sugar and cocoa.

Drop by the teaspoon onto cookie sheet and shape into cones. Bake 25-30 minutes, or until outsides are firm to the touch and insides are still soft. These kisses are very fragile, so handle with TLC until cool!

Serving: 1 Cookie	Calories: 20	Protein: 1 gm
Calories from Fat: 2	Total Fat: 0.5 gm	Dietary Fiber: 0 gm
Saturated Fat: 0 gm	Carbs: 4 gm	Sodium: 10 mg
Component of Fat: 12%	Cholesterol: 0 mg	Calcium: 1 mg

Indian Apple Pudding

SERVES 6

2 cups skim milk
$^1/_3$ cup yellow cornmeal
pinch of salt
$^3/_4$ cup molasses
2 teaspoons cinnamon
1 egg
2 cups peeled and thinly
   sliced apples, cut into
   small pieces
$^1/_2$ cup cold skim milk

Preheat oven to 325°. Spray a 2-quart baking dish with non-stick oil.

Scald 2 cups milk over medium-high heat. While stirring, slowly add cornmeal, salt, molasses and cinnamon. Remove from heat.

Beat egg, then whisk into pudding Stir in apple pieces. Pour into baking dish and bake 1 hour. Pour $^1/_2$-cup milk over pudding, without stirring, and bake another $1^1/_2$-2 hours. Serve pudding hot with non-fat whipped cream or frozen yogurt.

Serving: 1/6 Recipe	Calories: 225	Protein: 5 gm
Calories from Fat: 12	Total Fat: 1 gm	Dietary Fiber: 2 gm
Saturated Fat: 0.5 gm	Carbs: 50 gm	Sodium: 89 mg
Component of Fat: 5%	Cholesterol: 38 mg	Calcium: 242 mg

Plums in Sweet Vermouth Sauce

Keep a bottle of inexpensive vermouth available for cooking.
It is just as flavorful as "cooking vermouth" and half the price.

2 lbs. fresh plums
$1/_2$ cup packed brown sugar
$1/_2$ cup vermouth
pinch of salt
$1/_4$ cup water

MAKES 3 CUPS

Concasse plums as follows: Boil a pot of water. With a paring knife, score an "X" in top and bottom of plums. Place in boiling water 5 minutes, then remove with slotted spoon. The skins will peel off easily.

Cut plums into large bite-sized pieces. Combine in saucepan with brown sugar, vermouth, salt and water. Cook over medium-high heat, stirring occasionally, for about 25 minutes, until plums are tender and sauce thickens. If needed, add more water.

Serving: 1/2 Cup	Calories: 172	Protein: 2 gm
Calories from Fat: 8	Total Fat: 1 gm	Dietary Fiber: 2 gm
Saturated Fat: 0 gm	Carbs: 38 gm	Sodium: 28 mg
Component of Fat: 5%	Cholesterol: 0 mg	Calcium: 23 mg

Plums in Sweet Vermouth Sauce are excellent served over cheesecake, frozen yogurt, rice pudding, or enjoyed solo in all its splendor. Best of all, this rich sauce has almost no fat!

Lemon Cheesecake

Cheesecake Crust:
2 cups sugared graham
    cracker crumbs
2 tablespoons canola oil
1 tablespoon lemon juice

Cheesecake Filling:
3 eggs
16 oz. light cream cheese,
    softened
16 oz. non-fat sour cream
$1/2$ cup part-skim Ricotta
    cheese, well drained
2 tablespoons cornstarch
$1^1/_2$ cups sugar
2 tablespoons lemon juice
1 teaspoon finely grated
    lemon rind
2 teaspoons vanilla extract
pinch of salt

SERVES 12

Combine crust ingredients in mixing bowl. Spray 9-inch spring-mold pan with non-stick oil. Press crust mixture into bottom of pan and $2^1/_2$ inches up the sides. Bake in 375° oven 3 minutes, then chill.

In blender, whip eggs, cream cheese, sour cream, Ricotta and cornstarch. Pour into mixing bowl and stir in remaining ingredients. Beat until completely smooth. Pour into crust and bake at 325° until just set, about 50 minutes. Turn off oven, leaving cheesecake inside, for 1 hour more. Cool completely at room temperature, then chill at least 6 hours before serving. Garnish with fresh fruit.

Serving: 1 Piece		Calories: 345	Protein: 10 gm
Calories from Fat: 98		Total Fat: 11 gm	Dietary Fiber: 1 gm
Saturated Fat: 5.5 gm		Carbs: 50 gm	Sodium: 358 mg
Component of Fat: 29%		Cholesterol: 75 mg	Calcium: 128 mg

Chocolate Needham Squares

1 cup cold mashed
  potatoes
1 cup powdered sugar
2 cups shredded coconut
1½ teaspoons vanilla
¼ teaspoon salt
4 squares semi-sweet
  baking chocolate

MAKES 64 PIECES

Whip together mashed potatoes, sugar, shredded coconut, vanilla and salt. Blend well and press into an 8-inch square non-stick pan.

Boil water in bottom pan of double boiler. In the top pan, melt chocolate. Pour melted chocolate over needham mixture. When chocolate begins to cool, mark into 1-inch squares. Repeat marking through cooling process and needhams will not fracture when divided. Cool at room temperature.

Serving: 1 Square
Calories from Fat: 18
Saturated Fat: 1.5 gm
Component of Fat: 41%

Calories: 41
Total Fat: 2 gm
Carbs: 6 gm
Cholesterol: 0 mg

Protein: 0 gm
Dietary Fiber: 1 gm
Sodium: 18 mg
Calcium: 5 mg

Seasonal Preserves & Jams

CONTENTS

ABOUT CANNING

Jars: Use only properly sealed canning jars with rubber airtight seals or a two-piece metal screw-down lid. Check against defects such as chips or cracks. Jars must be sterilized in boiling water or dishwasher, and filled while still hot.

Packing Jars: Fill while preserves and jar are very hot, leaving $1/4$ to $1/2$-inch headroom. Before sealing, release trapped air by running a butter knife or spatula down the insides of the jar. Wipe top of jar clean before sealing.

Canning at a High Altitude: Increase processing time in boiling water bath by 1 minute for every 1000 feet above sea level.

Cherry Jam

3 lbs. ripe cherries
1 cup water
1 cup orange juice
1 tablespoon lemon juice
3 cups sugar

MAKES 4 PINTS
Read about canning on page 150

Cut cherries into quarters and discard pits. Bring cherries, water and juices to a full boil. Simmer for 20 minutes. Stir in sugar until completely dissolved. Taste, add sugar or lemon juice as desired. Continue stirring and simmer 30 minutes. Pour into hot jars, seal.

Place jars on rack in boiler half-filled with boiling water, leaving space between jars. Add boiling water to cover jars 2 inches above their tops. Bring to a boil, cover, and process 10 minutes. Using tongs, lift jars (not by the lids) and set on towels with several inches between them to cool.

Serving: 2 Tablespoons	Calories: 53	Protein: 0 gm
Calories from Fat: 2	Total Fat: 0 gm	Dietary Fiber: 1 gm
Saturated Fat: 0 gm	Carbs: 13 gm	Sodium: 0 mg
Component of Fat: 3%	Cholesterol: 0 mg	Calcium: 4 mg

Plum Jelly

4 lbs. small red plums
3 cups water
3 cups sugar
1 pouch (3 oz.) liquid
    fruit pectin

MAKES 4 PINTS

Wash, remove pits, and quarter plums. Boil in water for 40 minutes. Skim froth. Press pulp through fine sieve or jelly bag, discarding skins.

Mix pulp with sugar and pectin, dissolve well. Return to pot and boil for 3 minutes. Skim froth. Pour into hot sterilized jelly jars, leaving $1/2$-inch headroom.

Seal with a two-piece metal screw-down lid according to manufacturer's directions.

Serving: 2 Tablespoons	Calories: 59	Protein: 0 gm
Calories from Fat: 2	Total Fat: 0 gm	Dietary Fiber: 0 gm
Saturated Fat: 0 gm	Carbs: 15 gm	Sodium: 0 mg
Component of Fat: 3%	Cholesterol: 0 mg	Calcium: 1 mg

There are many varieties of plums. Fresh eating plums such as the *Italian prune*, the Japanese *Santa Rosa* and the yellow-green *Kelsey* are commonly seen in supermarkets. The *Damson*, a small, oval, blue-black plum is tart but has an excellent flavor for sweetened preserves or pies. In Eastern Europe plums are fermented to make slivovitz brandy.

Brandied Peach Preserves

4 lbs. peaches,
   ripe but firm
2 cups sugar
3 cups water
$^1/_2$ cup brandy

MAKES 4 PINTS
Read about canning on page 150

Rub fuzz off peaches with a coarse towel. Rinse, cut in half lengthwise and pit. Combine sugar and water in a large pot, and cook into a syrup. Add peaches, simmer 10 minutes. Remove peaches with slotted spoon and place in sterilized jars. Pour 2 tablespoons brandy over peaches in each jar. Fill jar with hot syrup and seal.

Place jars on rack in boiler half-filled with boiling water, leaving space between jars. Add boiling water to cover jars 2 inches above their tops. Bring to a boil, cover, and process 15 minutes. Using tongs, lift out jars (not by their lids) and set on towels with several inches between them to cool.

Serving: 1/2 Cup	Calories: 163	Protein: 1 gm
Calories from Fat: 1	Total Fat: 0 gm	Dietary Fiber: 2 gm
Saturated Fat: 0 gm	Carbs: 38 gm	Sodium: 2 mg
Component of Fat: 0%	Cholesterol: 0 mg	Calcium: 7 mg

Tomato Preserves

2 lbs. red or yellow
    tomatoes
$^1/_2$ cup sugar
1 lemon, thinly sliced and
    seeded
1 tablespoon grated fresh
    ginger

MAKES 2 PINTS

Scald and skin tomatoes. Place in bowl, cover with sugar and refrigerate 12 hours. Drain juice and boil it down until thickened. Add tomatoes, lemon and ginger. Simmer for 20 minutes. Pack in hot sterilized jars, leaving $^1/_2$-inch headroom. Seal jars.

Place jars on rack in boiler half-filled with boiling water, leaving space between them. Add boiling water to cover jars 2 inches above their tops. Bring to a boil, cover, and process 10 minutes. Using tongs, lift jars (not by the lids) and set on towels with several inches between them to cool.

Serving: 1/2 Cup	Calories: 76	Protein: 1 gm
Calories from Fat: 4	Total Fat: 0 gm	Dietary Fiber: 1 gm
Saturated Fat: 0 gm	Carbs: 19 gm	Sodium: 11 mg
Component of Fat: 4%	Cholesterol: 0 mg	Calcium: 14 mg

Sweet Pepper Marmalade

12 red bell peppers
$^1/_4$ cup olive oil
5 cloves minced garlic
1 tablespoon powdered
    ginger
$^1/_2$ cup orange juice
1 tablespoon lemon juice
3 tablespoons sugar
1 tablespoon brown sugar
1 teaspoon ground black
    pepper

MAKES 3 PINTS

Clean and seed peppers. Dice into small pieces, about $^1/_4$-inch square.

Heat oil over medium-low heat in large pan. Add garlic and cook 5 minutes. Add peppers, stir well and cover. Cook 10 minutes. Add remaining ingredients, mix, cover, and continue to cook 25 minutes.

Remove cover from pan, reduce heat to low. Stirring frequently, cook 1 hour. Serve warm or pack in jars. Store in refrigerator.

Serving: 2 Tablespoons	Calories: 22	Protein: 0 gm
Calories from Fat: 11	Total Fat: 2 gm	Dietary Fiber: 1 gm
Saturated Fat: 0 gm	Carbs: 3 gm	Sodium: 1 mg
Component of Fat: 44%	Cholesterol: 0 mg	Calcium: 5 mg

Pickled Beets

2 lbs. peeled and thinly
   sliced beets
2 quarts water
2 tablespoons pickling
   salt
$1\frac{1}{2}$ cups vinegar
$1\frac{1}{2}$ cups water
1 cup sugar
1 teaspoon peppercorns
1 teaspoon mustard seed

MAKES 4 PINTS
Read about canning on page 150.

Boil beets 10 minutes in 2 quarts water with pickling salts. Drain and pack in sterilized jars. Boil all other ingredients together, and simmer for 3 minutes. Pour hot liquid over beets, leaving $\frac{1}{2}$-inch headroom, seal.

Place jars on rack in boiler half-filled with boiling water, leaving space between jars. Add boiling water to cover jars 2 inches above their tops. Bring to a boil, cover and process 10 minutes. Using tongs, lift jars (not by the lids) and set on towels with several inches between them to cool.

Serving: 1 Cup	Calories: 154	Protein: 2 gm
Calories from Fat: 3	Total Fat: 0.5 gm	Dietary Fiber: 4 gm
Saturated Fat: 0 gm	Carbs: 39 gm	Sodium: 99 mg
Component of Fat: 2%	Cholesterol: 0 mg	Calcium: 24 mg

Fireplace cookery in early New England history was strictly women's work. Vegetables such as turnips, pumpkin, beans, beets, dried beans and corn were usually cooked together in a heavy iron kettle weighing about 50 pounds. The hot kettle had to be carefully maneuvered on and off the open fire, which required both strength and skill.

Bread & Butter Pickles

5 quarts thickly sliced
    pickling cucumbers
1/4 cup pickling salt
4 cups vinegar
1 quart sliced onion
1 cup honey
2 tablespoons mustard
    seed
1 tablespoon celery seed
1 tablespoon turmeric

MAKES 6 PINTS
Read about canning on page 150

Cover cucumbers with cold water, add salt. Let sit 2 hours, drain and rinse well. Put in large pot with all other ingredients and cook over medium-high heat 30 minutes. Pack cucumbers and liquid in sterilized jars, seal.

Place jars on rack in boiler half-filled with boiling water, leaving space between jars. Add boiling water to cover jars 2 inches above their tops. Bring to a boil, cover, and process 10 minutes. Using tongs, lift jars (not by the lids) and set on towels with several inches between them to cool.

Serving: 2 Tablespoons	Calories: 22	Protein: 0 gm
Calories from Fat: 1	Total Fat: 0 gm	Dietary Fiber: 1 gm
Saturated Fat: 0 gm	Carbs: 5 gm	Sodium: 3 mg
Component of Fat: 5%	Cholesterol: 0 mg	Calcium: 11 mg

Curried Apricot Chutney

2 cups water
2 cups chopped dried
   apricots
$\frac{1}{2}$ cup onion, chopped
   fine
$\frac{1}{2}$ cup sugar
$1\frac{1}{2}$ cups cider vinegar
1 teaspoon ginger
2 teaspoons curry powder
1 teaspoon cinnamon
pinch of salt
1 cup golden raisins

MAKES 2 PINTS
Read about canning on page 150

Simmer water, apricots, onions and sugar 30 minutes. In a separate pan, cook vinegar and spices over medium heat for 5 minutes. Combine both mixtures with raisins. Pack in hot sterilized jars and seal.

Place jars on rack in boiler half-filled with boiling water, leaving space between jars. Add boiling water to cover jars 2 inches above their tops. Bring to a boil, cover and process 10 minutes. Using tongs, lift jars (not by the lids) and set on towels with several inches between them to cool.

Serving: 2 Tablespoons	Calories: 52	Protein: 1 gm
Calories from Fat: 1	Total Fat: 0 gm	Dietary Fiber: 0 gm
Saturated Fat: 0 gm	Carbs: 14 gm	Sodium: 6 mg
Component of Fat: 1%	Cholesterol: 0 mg	Calcium: 8 mg

Fresh Lemonade Syrup

Serve this syrup with tall glasses of ice water for perfect lemonade.

2 cups sugar
1 cup water
rind of 2 lemons, cut in
    thin strips
juice of 6 freshly squeezed
    lemons

MAKES 2¹/₂ CUPS SYRUP

Boil sugar, water and lemon rind together for 10 minutes. Cool to room temperature and add freshly squeezed lemon juice. Strain the syrup and store in a glass jar. Syrup will keep at least 3 weeks in the refrigerator.

To serve lemonade: Chill tall glasses, fill with ice. Set out ice water in pitcher and lemonade syrup in creamer-type server. Everyone can now prepare their own lemonade to taste. Place glasses on small doilies alongside a tall stirring spoon and straw to complete the setting for a perfect summer cooler.

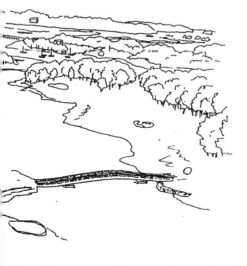

Serving: 4 Tablespoons
Calories from Fat: 0
Saturated Fat: 0 gm
Component of Fat: 0%

Calories: 163
Total Fat: 0 gm
Carbs: 43 gm
Cholesterol: 0 mg

Protein: 0 gm
Dietary Fiber: 0 gm
Sodium: 2 mg
Calcium: 6 mg

Wentworth By The Sea Golf Club
New Castle, New Hampshire

The Coastal New England Cooking Series

NOTES ON USING THESE BOOKS

Each book is oriented to take advantage of the fresh produce of the season. Try to buy locally grown produce in the freshest condition possible. Locally grown food not only has the best flavor and greatest amount of vitamins, but it is economical as well.

To allow for a variety of foods, fruits and vegetables which freeze or dry well are also used in their preferred state of storage. Fresh produce, fish, grains, flours, dairy and beans provide a diverse and healthy diet, without the animal fats and other problems associated with red meat.

Non-fat and low-fat dairy products are readily available and provide calcium, protein, nutrition and flavor, with much less fat. They are an excellent substitute to whole milk products. Low-sodium tomato products and bouillon broth are occasionally used, substitution of regular items will simply increase sodium.

Non-stick oil spray is intended to mean a non-fat vegetable oil spray. When it is used in addition to a cooking oil, it allows the use of less oil.

The nutritional analysis assumes a "pinch of salt" or "salt to taste" is .05 teaspoons of salt. The same measurement is used for other spices as well.

Preheating the oven or broiler takes only 15 minutes. Save electricity: don't warm your appliances until 15 minutes before they will be used.

COASTAL NEW ENGLAND   SUMMERTIME COOKING

Following the Guidelines of
The American Heart Association

A complete statement of the Guidelines of the American Heart Association can be obtained by contacting your local chapter. For healthy adults, this cookbook presents a simple approach to following these guidelines. Adding together the various nutritional components of your meals will help provide a better understanding of your diet.

By reducing meat and chicken, a large amount of saturated fat (an artery-damaging fat) will be replaced by more healthful protein and fats. Saturated fats should be limited to 10% of calories. All animal products, including cheese, also contain cholesterol, and their use should be limited.

Polyunsaturated fats (found in salmon, leafy vegetables and seeds), and especially the Omega-3 fatty acids, are believed to have an anticlotting agent helpful in preventing heart attack and stroke. Monounsaturated fats are often praised for not raising the damaging LDL cholesterol, and are found in olive and canola oils.

Keep the amount of pre-prepared foods to a minimum. Enjoy a wide variety of fresh foods with a broad range of their natural vitamins, minerals and nutrients. Fresh fruits and vegetables can be eaten regularly, without restriction.

Total fat intake should not exceed 30% of the calories consumed. Even polyunsaturated and monounsaturated fats should be consumed in limited quantities, and will achieve the greatest benefit if they replace, not supplement, the saturated fats presently consumed.

Following the Guidelines of
The American Heart Association

(cont.) Carbohydrates should make up at least 50-60% of the diet. This includes vegetables, fruits, grains, flours and beans. The American Heart Association recommends calories be adjusted to achieve and maintain a healthy body weight.

Make a habit of reaching for fruit or naturally sweetened products. The recipes in this book offer a reasonable alternative to the traditional high-fat and caloric desserts, but they are not intended to be eaten everyday or in volumes greater than the proportions shown.

Sodium intake should follow the advice of your physician, or be limited to an average of 3 grams per day. Recipes in this book can be made without salt or allow for "salt to taste." The desire for salty foods is acquired, you can become more sensitive to the taste of salt by slowly reducing its volume. Try using sea salt in small amounts, it is more flavorful and contains minerals not present in table salt.

Limit alcohol to a maximum of one or two drinks per day. And...

Exercise! It makes your body work better, and feel better, too.

Suggested Kitchen Tools, Utensils and Stock Items

Kitchen Tools and Utensils:
Set of whisks in assorted sizes
Slotted spoon and spatula
Blender
Double boiler
Non-stick skillet and frying pans in assorted sizes with lids
Oven casseroles with lids
Non-aluminum pots, pans and containers
Rolling pin
Large stainless steel bowl for mixing bread doughs
Pie pans, regular and deep-dish

Stock Items:
A good variety of spices, fresh fruits and vegetables
Non-stick, non-fat vegetable oil spray
Canola, olive and safflower oils
Vegetable bouillon cubes or powder
Skim milk
Non-fat powdered milk (to enrich skim milk)
Low-fat buttermilk
Non-fat plain yogurt, cottage cheese and cream cheese
Low-fat and part-skim cheese products

Measurements

a pinch.................................. $^{1}/_{20}$ teaspoon
3 teaspoons............................ 1 tablespoon
4 tablespoons......................... $^{1}/_{4}$ cup
16 tablespoons........................ 1 cup
2 cups.................................... 1 pint
4 cups.................................... 1 quart
4 quarts................................. 1 gallon
8 quarts................................. 1 peck
16 ounces............................... 1 pound
8 ounces liquid....................... 1 cup
1 ounce liquid........................ 2 tablespoons

Substitutions

1 tablespoon cornstarch............ 2 T. flour or 2 tsp. quick-cooking tapioca
2 teaspoons arrowroot.............. 1 tablespoon cornstarch
1 teaspoon baking powder .... $^{1}/_{4}$ tsp. baking soda + $^{1}/_{2}$ tsp. cream of tartar
$^{1}/_{2}$ cup brown sugar.................. 2 T. molasses in $^{1}/_{2}$ cup granulated sugar
$^{3}/_{4}$ cup cracker crumbs.............. 1 cup bread crumbs
1 tablespoon fresh herbs........... 1 teaspoon dried herbs
1 small clove garlic................... $^{1}/_{8}$ teaspoon garlic powder
1 fresh onion.......................... 2 T. instant minced onion, rehydrated
1 cup whole milk... .... $^{1}/_{2}$ c. skimmed evaporated milk + $^{1}/_{2}$ c. water
1 cup buttermilk...................... 1 cup non-fat plain yogurt

PRINTED IN THE U.S.A.

20% TOTAL RECYCLED FIBER
20% POST-CONSUMER FIBER